City Preaching

Sermons on Death and Resurrection

in

Baltimore

Robert P. Hoch

Parson's Porch Books
www.parsonsporchbooks.com

City Preaching: Sermons on Death and Resurrection in Baltimore
ISBN: 9781949888867
Copyright © 2018 by Robert P. Hoch

All rights reserved. No part of this book may be reproduced or transmitted in any form or by any means, electronic or mechanical, including photocopying, recording, or by any information storage and retrieval system, without permission in writing from the publisher.

Unless otherwise indicated, Scripture quotations are from The New Revised Standard Version Bible, copyright © 1989 National Council of the Churches of Christ in the United States of America. Used by permission. All rights reserved.

To my Mother

Contents

Acknowledgments 9
Introduction 11
Chapter One 17
   Because of What She Said
Chapter Two 24
   #We Stand with Orlando
Chapter Three 30
   You've Changed
Chapter Four 37
   By Chance It Happened
Chapter Five 44
   What Happens in Vegas
Chapter Six 51
   The Art of the Deal
Chapter Seven 59
   A Prayer with Punch
Chapter Eight 66
   An Opportunity to Testify
Chapter Nine 73
   A Taste of Freedom
Chapter Ten 80
   For the Time Being
Chapter Eleven 87
   Pick of the Litter
Chapter Twelve 88
   Growing Like Weeds

Chapter Thirteen 100
    Do Not Cling to Me
Chapter Fourteen 106
    Beyond Our Wants
Chapter Fifteen 114
    Mostly Healthy
Chapter Sixteen 122
    Seven Years Old
Chapter Severnteen 127
    Learning a New Song
Chapter Eighteen 134
    Ready for Christmas?
Chapter Nineteen 141
    Fevers Relieved

In a world typified by death, what brings notice that something transformative is on the horizon is life in the face of death, life even after death, life in spite of death, life that unlocks the doors and thus breaks the power of death. What the purveyors of death notice is defiant life. It is resurrection that frightens them. . . .

Only life can conquer death.

Brian K. Blount, *Invasion of the Dead: Preaching Resurrection*

Acknowledgments

It is with deep gratitude that I acknowledge those who have been significant in my preaching life. Actually, there are many, too many to name. We always fail to give thanks adequately, which suggests not so much that we're thankless (except when we are) but that grace abounds. Perhaps surprisingly, I feel a debt to the library, St. Mary's Theological Library in particular. Good theological books, solid scholarly work, a space dedicated to study — these quicken my otherwise dull mind. Without that little sanctuary to the north, I don't know how I could preach, week in and week out.

And, of course, my gratitude to the congregation of First & Franklin Presbyterian Church cannot be underestimated: without your questions, heart-ache, your hopes and dedication, your physical and intellectual presence, these sermons would not exist — or perhaps we would not exist without one another. Some of you, as I write, I can see you, where you sit in the sanctuary or up in the choir loft. Many of you will know not only the words, but the feeling of that moment. Thank you for giving me the privilege and responsibility of preaching in this city — we have been called together "for such an hour as this."

In particular, I am grateful to Beth Seeley. Beth told me once that she prefers to work behind the scenes, or, as in the case of this work, in the margins. As you read this collection, you will not see her edits or suggestions, but be assured that she was there all along. . . .

Dr. John McLucas, long-time member of First & Franklin Presbyterian Church, probably heard almost every sermon in this collection. He also connected with me in the call process, which led me to accept the invitation to serve as First & Franklin's pastor. His e-mails were always eloquent, always generous, and always grace-filled. He once referred to me as his "imaginary friend" — I am so glad that today we are real friends. It's the way, as my real friend, you walk Gabriel home from church. The way, as real friends, we share a wee dram after a long meeting. The way, as real friends, we drink Root Beer together, which is just as satisfying, only in a different way. Thank you for reading an early draft of this book — you possess the uncommon ability to bring out the best not only in situations but in people. I am glad I can count myself as one of your real people! As some wise soul once said, "Who has more fun than we do?"

Of course, my family. Our children, Gwendoline, Imogen, Gabriel, and Iris, have heard many of these sermons, some of them twice. Occasionally (not every Saturday) I will "read out" a sermon for our "congregation" at home.

City Preaching

Iris, five-years old, must have concluded that the Saturday night rehearsal was now "old" news because on Sunday morning, hearing the same sermon again, she whipped around to her mother and said indignantly, "Daddy's already preached this one!" My children deserve an extra reward in heaven, for perseverance through sermonic thick and sermonic thin!

And last but not least, Rebecca, my spouse and best friend: thank you for asking on Saturday night, "Do you really want to say that?"

Thanks be to God!

Introduction

Weather fronts form clouds, endlessly varied and dynamic; likewise, sermons form an identity, a congregation or better movements. What carries each along is beyond our engineering, beyond our best guesses: "The wind blows where it chooses, and you hear the sound of it, but you do not know where it comes from or where it goes" (John 3:8). Gusts of invisible wind whip trees into leafy clouds of whirling unrest, into the twirling dervishes of silver and green. Clouds form, dissolve, scatter, collide, rise, condense into rain or snow or hail or sleet; or they thunder with electric storm, strobing with unpredictable light.

The psalmist sings of God's Word employing natural, and largely (and humanly) uncontrollable, phenomena: "The Lord sends out his command to the earth; God's word runs swiftly; he gives snow like wool; he scatters frost like ashes. He hurls down hail like crumbs — who can stand before his cold? He sends out his word, and melts them; he makes his wind blow, and the waters flow" (Psalm 147:15-18). These natural phenomena, fire, hail, snow, and frost "fulfill God's command" (Psalm 148:8). Powerful, frequently destructive powers belong to God's sovereign command: "You set the beams of your chambers on the waters, you make the clouds your chariot, you ride on the wings of the wind. You make the winds your messengers, fire and flame your ministers" (Psalm 104:3-4).

Out of a whirlwind, God speaks to Job. If God speaks out of the whirlwind, maybe the preacher speaks out of an ache or an itch or a hunch. A prophetic "woe" and "fire in my bones" exists in the vocality of the preacher. Dip each word of the sermon into your heart, advises George Herbert, poet and priest. Our preaching, he says, should not only be careful in exposition, but it should be heart-deep. It's not enough to exposit a text (though that is important). Herbert encourages something more than "crumbling the text into small parts" which he likens to preaching a dictionary rather than the proclamation of Scripture. Through our engagement with Scripture as Scripture, the text gets resuscitated with the flesh, skin, and crucially breath of congregational life within the sermonic moment.[1] We preach somewhat analogously to the way the psalmist prays, with everything we've got, experience, skill, loneliness, and especially things that we do not know (and have not got), but which our God knows and coveys in sighs, gasps, and song of the Spirit.

---

[1] George Herbert, *The Temple and the Country Parson* (Boston: James B. Dow, 1842 [1652]), excerpted in Richard Lischer, ed., *The Company of Preachers: Wisdom on Preaching* (Grand Rapids: William B. Eerdmans Publishing Company, 2002), 66-7.

So sometimes, the sermon (and the preacher) gasps for God's word. This collection of sermons represents my best work, or my best "gasp" for God's Word. Preaching takes us all through a crucible of sorts but the last few years have been especially trying. I've spoken to colleagues who have been preaching for decades and they too speak of our time as a uniquely difficult season for the North American pulpit. This collection reflects these times. Between 2016 and 2017, we witnessed innumerable mass shootings, one of the most divisive presidential elections in history, white terrorism in Charlottesville, and a nearly constant barrage of abuse from the White House. Not least, there is a sense that ideologues are attempting to hijack theological language for xenophobic propaganda. That being the case, there's a scrappy element to the preaching you will find here.

You may wonder if there was any grand design to the selection of texts or sermonic themes. If there is, it might be a theological bent toward resurrection. But you will see lots of death in these sermons. Lots. I hope you will also see glimpses of seriously imaginable resurrection. What does it mean to preach resurrection in a society where death seems as if it is the only game in town? "Preaching resurrection is not just for Easter anymore," writes Brian Blount. "We must find a way to image [resurrection], to affirm our expectation for it, and to find ways to recast it in contemporary symbolism that connects with our contemporary age."[2] Probably without realizing it in a deliberate way, I have sought to tap into the resurrection imagination as a form of living defiance, joyfully existing and testifying in the space of death dealing powers. I preach poetically, but I also aim to "clothe" our experience of resurrection with recognizable garments from our social, emotional, and political lives. Look for the ordinary bush — and *almost* commonplace people — alight with holy fire.

Sermonic Texts and Setting

Ordinarily, a sermon emerges from a close reading of a Scripture text. Usually, I select the text (one primary text for each sermon) from the Revised Common Lectionary. There are exceptions. This volume includes a collection of sermons based on the Book of Ruth, which was part of a summer series from Old Testament books. Beginning in the fall of 2016, and continuing throughout the year, I settled down and preached from one text in the lectionary. For a short season, I chose the assigned text from the Book of Psalms as my primary text. You will find two "topical sermons" which means that they do not engage in a close reading of the text but instead follow broad

---

[2] Brian K. Blount, *Invasion of the Dead: Preaching Resurrection* (Louisville: Westminster John Knox Press, 2014), 27.

themes of Christian faith — one is an ordination sermon for a former student and the other was a somewhat whimsical sermon addressed to my son, Gabriel, a few weeks before his seventh birthday. The sermons are arranged chronologically, from June of 2016 to December 2017. There is a gap in time between the final sermon of 2017 and the sermon that concludes this collection, dated May of 2018, which serves as something like an epilogue (more on that below).

The sermons themselves grow out of a city and a nation in turmoil. Specifically, the collection comes principally from congregational life in the urban, eclectic, somewhat gritty, and somewhat privileged Mt. Vernon neighborhood of Baltimore. First & Franklin is proud of its courageous pulpit, its music, its historic role in Baltimore. General George Washington gave Rev. Patrick Allison (1740-1802), the founding pastor of this congregation, a walking stick. On it, the congregation has engraved the names of their pastors, from the founding of the church to present day. A walking stick serves as a potent symbol because it speaks to the pilgrimage journey of the life of faith. We know most of Jesus' life through the walk-path. Israel's journey, too, is conceived as a pilgrimage through desert and exile. Its connection with George Washington, our first president, suggests our congregation is something like a midwife to our national convulsions (contractions), always in the labor for new life and hope. Our congregation has, in its memory, a sense of its national vocation as Matthew's "city on a hill" (Matthew 5:14).

The present congregation is housed in an architectural style known variously as Lancet Gothic, Gothic Revival, or (my favorite) Flamboyant Gothic. It was built between 1854 and 1859, with its steeple being completed in 1879. At 273-feet, the steeple can be seen from a couple of miles away. It self-describes as a destination church. Mount Vernon continues to be the LGBTQ neighborhood of Baltimore. We are a congregation that is proud of our role in the fight for LGBTQ inclusion and marriage equality. It is also a church in the middle of a city that has for several decades been predominantly black. While it is in a relatively wealthy neighborhood, it is within a few blocks of some of Baltimore's boarded up neighborhoods. In truth, that is the case for many churches in Baltimore: the poorest communities are within a few minutes' walking distance from the wealthiest and vice versa.

Some of those reading this book will be members of this community. They will hear some of the sermons twice, first in the heat of the moment — and some of these sermons flared hot with the hour — but now, cooler to the touch, in recollection. About that heat . . . one of my earliest memories of First & Franklin was walking up the back alley, seeing a swarm of police helicopters buzzing over the courthouse. It was the day that all charges were dropped against the police officers involved in Freddie Gray's death. They were monitoring the courthouse, presumably in case of social unrest. That's where they were physically. But to my eye, it almost appeared as if they were wasps, the sound of them like a swarm of stirred up hornets, hovering around our steeple. It left a lasting impression on me. I don't remember the sermon from that Sunday. But in some way, that social unrest adds a peculiar complexion to this collection of sermons, irrespective of the content of each one. Indeed, the second sermon of this collection was delivered one week after the Pulse Shooting in Orlando, Florida. I know because I was formally installed as pastor on the day of the mass shooting. The next-to-last sermon of this collection was preached on Christmas Eve of 2017, concluding one of the bloodiest years in Baltimore's history. Urban poverty, gun violence, police corruption, racial segregation, a city starved of funds for its schools and infrastructure, a net population decline: that's the city, or at least part of it.

But something else wends its way through these sermons, not exactly a sermonic theme, but a physical symbol. Those who heard these sermons will remember the purple ribbons representing lives lost in our city, even if they have forgotten the sermons. Beginning in April of 2017, our church adopted a practice of memorializing each victim of homicide in the City of Baltimore with a purple ribbon. Every week we prayed; and every week, we tied a purple ribbon to the outside of the church, on Park Avenue. By the end of 2017, there were 343 purple ribbons, with the names of homicide victims listed nearby, alongside our church sanctuary.

In 2018, we decided to take these prayers on a pilgrimage to the offices of our state delegates and senators in Annapolis. We gave each representative the number of ribbons corresponding to the number of deaths in her or his district. Eventually, representatives and public officials visited our church and not only our church but especially the mothers of those who have died in our city. As a congregation, we looked on as one of the mothers of Baltimore's lost generation, Tanya Street, presented Darryl De Sousa, the newly appointed Police Commissioner, with a purple ribbon. She gave it to him in memory of her son and as a challenge to him to be a leader for positive change in our city.

The next time I saw De Sousa, it was in City Hall, where he was about to be confirmed. When he saw me, he asked, "Do you know what I have with me?"

"No," I admitted, "I don't."

He pulled a purple ribbon from his pocket — our prayers had migrated from a sanctuary of lament to a confirmation hearing, where women and men were confronted by the symbol of a mother's testimony, a symbol of her tears and her courage.

On May 15, 2018, not long after his confirmation hearing, De Sousa resigned amid a federal investigation into charges of tax evasion.

Sometimes we suspect that our prayers don't rise much higher than the ceiling. But I'm not so sure. The final sermon reflects on a Mother's Day luncheon we hosted at our church. It wasn't your traditional Mother's Day celebration; and you would perhaps prefer not to be on the invited guest list. Why? Our honored guests that Saturday were mothers who had lost their children to violence in our city. They came from all over Baltimore, but also from some of the most troubled parts of our city: Sandtown-Winchester, Brooklyn, Darley Park, Mondawmin, Johnston Square, among others. They came from all over and they filled our sanctuary not merely with their number but with their stories. They were and are the mothers of mostly young men, mostly African American families and neighborhoods. For over a year, we had prayed the names of Baltimore's dead. And then, in May, their mothers came to this house of worship. The final sermon in this collection, dated May 2018, recalls that occasion in this congregation's life.

Sermons and Reflections

One more thing . . . each chapter introduces the sermon with a brief reflection or recollection of that sermonic moment. It's not a sermon but it may be related. Few preachers have much opportunity, or perhaps even desire, to return to a sermon that's already been delivered, unless out of necessity. In a preacher's life, necessity usually means we've got short notice or our homiletical funds are running low; we pull something from the file, dust it off, and preach it again. It's more a convenience than a reflective exercise. But most preachers would probably say that even though it is a convenience, there is a kind of reflective exercise in that process, though we don't often come out and say so. Maybe we should.

Annie Dillard recommends that we read our rough drafts (and every sermon is really a rough draft) as if it were a dying patient: "I do not so much write a book as sit up with it, as with a dying friend. During visiting hours, I enter its room with dread and sympathy for its many disorders. I hold its hand and hope it will get better."[3]

Perhaps these sermonic efforts will get better, too.

Listen deeply, because as you listen to the ragged breathing of this collection, its frequent pauses for a sip of water to wet parched lips, you may realize that you are at an inflection point, suspended somewhere between life and death; listen generously and patiently because what is being given to you is as sacred as the first cries of an infant when it is born. Listen hopefully, because death will not have the last word.

---

[3] Annie Dillard, *The Writing Life* (New York: Harper Perennial, 1989), 52.

Chapter One

Because of What She Said

I preached the following sermon in a neighboring church in Baltimore. They had agreed to host the search committee of the First & Franklin Presbyterian Church, which had lined up what we call a "neutral pulpit" to hear the preaching of ministerial candidates. A few weeks later, the committee extended a call; apparently this message landed.

As I read Scripture, I often look for the way a text "pings" with something I see in our collective life. The text, to use a metaphor, acts as a lens which helps me to see connections or analogies or draw associations to the witness of Scripture itself. Being aware of Baltimore, Freddie Gray, the Sandtown-Winchester unrest of 2015, my imagination went to the way this text might be viewed as a bodycam, in which supposedly behind-the-scenes behavior is filmed or recorded for public consumption. It also spoke to me about the way gendered and racialized views silence the voice of the oppressed and marginalized. Perhaps that's where I think the "hook" for this text occurred: on the one hand, Mark gives us a bodycam glimpse of Jesus and we're seeing how he really is, which is to say the least, problematic; and, on the other hand, we get a paradoxical glimpse of how Jesus overcomes racial constructions of the world/gospel by himself being overcome by a Syrophoenician woman's clever testimony.

In Mark's gospel, she represents one of the few who really "get" Jesus – and perhaps the only one who gets the upper hand on Jesus. Usually, the disciples don't get Jesus; the demons "know" who he is, the Son of God, but are silenced; and the opponents of Jesus don't respond with awe or amazement when Jesus cures the leper but, immediately, set out to have Jesus arrested. So it goes. However, in this text, Jesus underlines *her words* as more powerful than his words. Mark's story suggests a quirky, even revelatory moment in the story of Jesus. It also gives us a glimpse into the distinctive character of women in the Gospel of Mark. One finds courage as well as ambivalence. The shorter version of Mark says that the women went away from the tomb and said nothing to anyone – but perhaps they were not silent for long. There is some glimpse of the unexpected power of women's testimony in the preaching of the Syrophoenician woman.

The story from our home, of my then 8-year old daughter Imogen, struck me as light hearted and yet apt. I'll let you read it on your own, but my own sense is that the gospel gives us the capacity to change the dynamics of the conversation. This is precisely what the Syrophoenician woman does in this text. Indeed, it must have struck Jesus as familiar, almost like looking into mirror and seeing a Syrophoenician woman's face speaking his own word to him! Indeed, whether the terms are those set by scarcity, or by fear, or by the force of raw power, Jesus proclaims the Rule of God, which is powerful to change the most elemental divisions between us into occasions for liberation joy — a joy that may initially strike us as a form of theological sass.

Sermon

> *From there, Jesus set out and went away to the region of Tyre. He entered a house and did not want anyone to know he was there. Yet he could not escape notice, but a woman whose little daughter had an unclean spirit immediately heard about him, and she came and bowed down at his feet. Now the woman was a Gentile, of Syrophoenician origin. She begged him to cast the demon out of her daughter. He said to her, "Let the children be fed first, for it is not fair to take the children's food and throw it to the dogs." But she answered him, "Sir, even the dogs under the table eat the children's crumbs." Then he said to her, "For saying that, you may go – the demon has left your daughter." So she went home, found the child lying on the bed, and the demon gone.*
>
> — Mark 7:24-37

You heard what Jesus said, didn't you? Or maybe I heard it wrong. Surely, Jesus doesn't say that kind of thing, does he? I never heard Jesus talk like that in Sunday School. Jesus said, "Let the little children come unto me." Jesus said, "Love one another." Jesus said, "Come to me all you who are weary and heavy burdened, and I will give you rest." Jesus said, "Blessed are the poor in spirit for they will inherit the kingdom of God."

Jesus says nice things. Jesus says things that make me feel good about myself. Jesus doesn't call people dogs. At least, I don't think he calls them dogs. And yet, I think, I do believe I heard Jesus call this woman, this woman who came to him for help, for her daughter, who fell at his feet, begging, I do think I distinctly remember hearing him call her a dog. Ouch. It's almost as if we have Jesus exposed by way of a biblical dash-cam, filming away, as the action unfolds. Unedited. Released to the public. All out there. This is not the Jesus we've come to expect. This is not the Jesus I thought I knew. Maybe this is not the Jesus we wanted to meet this morning, at church.

In fact, many of us, when we read this story want to clean it up. And the more you know about the historical context, the more you want to mop up the incriminating details. Jesus called her a dog. In fact, it was usual for Jews to call Gentiles, all Gentiles, dogs. My guess is that Syrophoenician folks had some choice descriptors for the Jews. That much is familiar. But none of that really excuses what we hear coming out of *Jesus'* mouth.

An historical note: dogs were unclean in the Jewish tradition. So, we're not talking about the kinds of animals we keep in our homes, the slobbering, smiling, puppy-brained animals we so love. These were snapping, scar-faced, snaggle tooth beasts, more likely to spend their days scavenging in the village dump than nestled in your lap. These were unclean animals.

There's not a lot you can do to minimize what Jesus says here, but that never stops us from trying. To this end, some write that Jesus was probably smiling when he called the woman a filthy, stinking, scavenging animal. In other words, maybe Jesus was speaking endearingly, as in, "You little beast, you!" Possible. But, ordinarily, terms of endearment require a familiarity that doesn't exist in today's text. Maybe we want this to say something other than its plain meaning.

Incidentally, if we ended up wanting to clean up this text, we would be in good company. Matthew and Luke both "clean" up the text in their own way. For Luke, that means dropping it altogether, perhaps because it was viewed as being too offensive for a Gentile audience. Matthew, for his part, kept it, but seems to stress Jesus' Jewishness. The woman, in Matthew's account, is a Canaanite — a religious rather than an ethnic group, as in Mark. And in Matthew, she also wisely recognizes Jesus as the Son of David. By contrast, in Mark's telling of the story, she's just a woman, a Syrophoenician woman with a demon possessed daughter, who heard about him, heard he was in town, heard reports, read her Twitter feed with the #healer-in-the-house, and came immediately. Crucially, in Matthew's account, it is the woman's *faith*, her trust rather than her retort, her snappy come back, that wins the day:

"O Woman, great is your faith!" (Matthew);

"For *saying* this, you may go your way" (Mark). [4]

So, in addition to saying things that Jesus isn't supposed to say, Mark's Jesus also gets one-upped, out-sassed, out-smarted by a stranger, by a

---

[4] C. S. Mann, *Mark: A New Translation with Introduction and Commentary* in The Anchor Bible Series, vol. 27 (New York: Doubleday & Company, 1986), 320-1.

Syrophoenician, by a woman no less. I'm not sure which presents the bigger problem here: what comes out of Jesus' mouth or the idea that someone, anyone, ever out-sasses the master of sass, namely God. God, the master of sass, who speaks, and the world becomes, out of the pin-point of nothing. A God whose hiccups create galaxies, and oceans; whose forgotten sigh gives birth to a sunrise like you've never seen before and you'll never see again. It would seem that God finishes all speaking . . . and after that, what could possibly be said that hasn't already been said? And certainly, that doesn't leave a lot of room for witty retorts.

And yet, this God we see in Jesus, master of sass, is out-sassed, out-smarted, and seemingly out-done by a stranger, by one the world would say is less, less because of her gender, less because of her ethnicity, less because she sits outside rather than on the inside. And Jesus, fully God and fully human, without separation or confusion, says, "You win. For what you have said, you win. Your words are true. You win. Go home now. You win. Your daughter is healed. For what you have said."

Apparently, there was something more to be said. And she says it. Like no one else in the Gospel of Mark.

You don't have to be a Bible scholar to know that Jesus always wins in verbal, word-to-word combat. Always. No exceptions. Well, except for today: for what she said, Jesus concedes. And Jesus' concession gives healing, restores health and wholeness. Usually, when I lose an argument, and this happens often, I sulk. I pout. But that's about it.

Not Jesus. Jesus admits she's right. For saying this, for saying that even the dogs eat the crumbs off the master's table, you win.

Maybe we don't understand precisely why Jesus said what he said, and we still struggle with what came out of Jesus' mouth — I think that's fair. But he can teach us to listen, to be willing to change our minds. Some people never change their minds. They say it's a matter of principle. But what if changing your mind is a symptom of active thought and maybe even a reflection of divine thought?

Jesus changes things all the time. Water into wine. A few loaves of bread and some fish — barely enough for a few — into a feast for five thousand. Jesus changes drifters and vagabonds into disciples. Jesus changes a tomb of death and defeat into a message of hope and victory. Jesus changes people and things . . . and perhaps Jesus changes his mind, too. By the way, not insignificantly, Jesus' active thought, namely, the change we see in his mind, leads to wholeness. Not capitulation. Jesus is practicing a different kind of politics here, a reign of God politics.

What if we say that this wasn't an accident? Perhaps, we caught a glimpse of a God who is too real to be hidden from the real world. Not six feet above contradiction, but a God waist deep in the world, pushing his way through streets flooded with pain, streets that carry as much debris as they do people, and sometimes it's hard to tell the debris from the people.

People, their dreams escaped like ghosts from the broken windows of lost opportunity and no opportunity, broken windows that never seem to get repaired. People so often pushed to the bottom and pushed to the back, that it's difficult to imagine anything else.

Maybe that's what stands out about this woman. Maybe she's been pushed to the bottom and pushed to the back so often she doesn't know anything different. It must have been a long road to that house where Jesus was staying. Try to imagine it. Maybe she looks a little like Rosa Parks, making her way to the front of the bus, maybe she looks like Sojourner Truth, and she's held her tongue so long in silence, but not anymore.

Maybe she's little Malala Yousafzai, and she's coming forward, a smart brown skinned girl, writing a blog, organizing, making speeches, fighting for the right of education for girls around the world — and she won't be stopped by threats, won't be muzzled by bullets, won't be silenced. And she's talking back. And the world took notice.

Because of what she said.

Maybe she counted every step, the Syrophoenician woman. And she held her breath. She didn't speak when she came into that house where Jesus had gone to hide, for a little privacy, to shelter from the street. She fell. Begged. Cried. Clasped Jesus' ankles. We see what she did. A mother pleading for her daughter. At this stage of the text, she moves and acts as if she were a victim, defined by her trouble. Mark tells us through all the pleading and begging, Jesus got the message. And then we hear how Jesus answered: "Let the children be fed first, for it is not right to take the children's bread and throw it to the dogs."

You notice the woman doesn't argue with Jesus. She might have done. We might wish she had. But sometimes a sharp insight wins more ground than a hard argument. The text gives us her come back, her sass: "Yes, Lord; yet even the dogs under the table eat the children's crumbs." She answered Jesus' ethnic smack down by claiming God's radical compassion — insisting on the compassion of God even in the face of its apparent absence. That is characteristic of faith. Her voice points to the justice of God she ultimately believed in, rather than the cruel answer she initially heard.

Turns out, she's got a voice. And a word. And she speaks it.

And equally important, God in Jesus Christ hears her voice in the depth of God's wisdom and love.

Jesus says, you're right. What you say is true. And what you claim from God is true of God and it is the truth of God. And what did Jesus give her for what she said? She went home. She found her daughter, a whole person again. Not a condition but child. Not a sick house but a home. Not a dog, but a mother with her daughter.

Because of what she said.

I don't know what you think of all this, but it makes me think about my own daughter. Imogen, eight-years-old, was running in the house the other day. She came around the corner of a book case like a miniature girl-version of Usain Bolt, the Olympic sprinter. In my biggest father of the house voice, I said, "Imogen, no running in the house!"

She stopped, rolled back on her heels, looked at me and said, "I'm not running. *I'm jogging!*"

Not bad! I really don't want her running in the house. But she what she said, the sass, the wit, the steely look in her eye. *That was good.* And I suppose I'd like our girls, and our children, to have a voice, to know how to answer back, to be "full of loud, in your face ideas."

Maybe that's what I'd like for myself, for the church. I don't want a church on a string, a puppet church jerked this way and that, in the name of principalities and powers, or some fossilized dogmatism. Maybe we need a little sass in our salvation. Need a little pertness in our prayer. We don't often think of prayer, of our talk with God as particularly sassy, but maybe it is. Maybe it's a bit like that.

Maybe when we come here, to this place, and we persist in believing in God's justice, insist on God's compassion, when the world and maybe even when our understandings of God seem to refuse that — but we continue, nevertheless, to testify to the God who saves, to the God who loosens tongues and opens eyes, testifying to the God in Jesus Christ who, ultimately, does all things well.

Maybe that's how we will be remembered. A sassy, pert little church. Full of loud, in your face, big ideas. Because of what we said to a world more familiar with famine than feast. Because of what we said in a world more likely to hurt than to heal. Because of what we said.

Even because of what we believed. About the God who came to us as bread. About God's justice, justice flowing like mighty waters. About God's healing. About God's unstoppable word of love. Speaking even now. The reign of God forming on our tongues and in our hearts.

An uprising against the disorder of the world. A little sass in our salvation, a little pertness in our testimony.

Remember sisters and brothers, Jesus commended her because of what she said.

Amen.

November 2015

Chapter Two

#We Stand with Orlando

I first became aware of the First & Franklin Church of Baltimore in the aftermath of the Freddie Gray unrest, in April of 2015. Along with the rest of the country, I watched in dismay as the uprising took over the streets of Baltimore. Little did I know that a year-and-a-half later, I would be saying, "I will" and "I do" as the moderator of Baltimore Presbytery installed me as this congregation's umpteenth pastor. It was over a year since the uprising, but the city still felt as if it were under siege. Police helicopters supplied a constant background noise, the high-pitched whir of their motors giving the city an ominous auditory signature. Early that summer, sitting on our back porch in the evening, we would be strafed by police search lights, aimed at us from helicopters patrolling overhead.

Some people have described the city as suffering from something like PTSD — it only needs a "trigger" to set it off. This was the city we moved to in late May of 2016. The police who had been involved in Freddie Gray's arrest hadn't yet been cleared of all wrong-doing, as they would be in August of that year. That was still ahead. On June 12, 2016, I was formally installed as the pastor of this historic church, one of the forerunners in the movement for the full inclusion of LGBTQ peoples in the life of the church. That same day, in Florida, Omar Mateen walked into a gay nightclub, The Pulse. By the time he finished shooting, forty-nine people were dead and fifty-three were wounded. The next evening our church, along with others in Baltimore City, gathered together at an abandoned parking lot off North Avenue, about a fifteen-minute walk from the church. We gathered to stand with those who had lost their lives. We also gathered to resist the wave of violent extremism taking over our streets. I took my then 10-year old daughter to the action. About twenty members of our church also turned out, ready to be counted in America's ongoing struggle against hate.

As you will see below, I was present for that assembly, but I was also on edge, thinking about potential reprisals. At the time, I had misgivings about sharing my personal fears of an attack from a rightwing group within the context of a sermon. Better to be courageous, fearless. But I'm not. Vulnerability (or transparency) in preaching is important, more important than the praise we get from being unalloyed heroes. The story of Elijah struck me as a potent reminder of our humanity, complicity, and the quiet strength of God's presence in times of earthquake, whirlwind, and fire.

Sermon

> *Then the word of the Lord came to him, saying, "What are you doing here, Elijah?" He answered, "I have been very zealous for the Lord, the God of Hosts; for the Israelites have forsaken your covenant, thrown down your altars, and killed your prophets with the sword. I alone am left, and they are seeking my life, to take it away." He said, "Go out and stand on the mountain before the Lord, for the Lord is about to pass by." Now there was a great wind, so strong that it was splitting mountains and breaking rocks in pieces before the Lord, but the Lord was not in the wind; and after the wind an earthquake, but the Lord was not in the earthquake; and after the earthquake a fire, but the Lord was not in the fire; and after the fire a sound of sheer silence. When Elijah heard it, he wrapped his face in his mantle and went out and stood at the entrance of the cave.*

—1 Kings 19:11-13a

On Monday, around twenty or so members of this church joined what looked like about a thousand people at the YNot Lot on 4 W. North Avenue. It was a candlelight vigil to express our solidarity with the victims of the shooting in Orlando.

It was a night of courage. Being real, as many of the speakers said. Real with our diversity, and real with our common humanity. Real about the things that divide us, and the things that unite us.

But as all this was going on, I couldn't help but notice movement in a building behind the stage. Two apartment windows were open, lights on. In the right window, I saw light and then someone looked through and then the light switched off, the apartment going dark. Then two or three men — it looked like men — two in front of the window, one standing behind the other two. They were watching vigil from the window.

And I couldn't tell, were they laughing? Listening? Jeering? One of them seemed to be trying to position something in the window — a camera, probably. That's what I thought. But part of me also wondered if it was something else. . . .

It's nothing, I thought to myself. But I pulled my daughter closer, just in case. It was only a whisper of fear, but I felt it. And if I felt it, my guess is that others were feeling it, too.

Ironic don't you think? That you or I would feel even a trace of fear for gathering in solidarity with LGBTQ people in this city or, perhaps, in this church. When marriage equality started happening, when the Supreme Court made its decision, it was as if the struggle had been won. It was a spectacular moment, wasn't it? It almost seemed like the struggle was finished.

But at around 2 a.m., on June 12, Omar Mateen walked into the Pulse Club in Orlando . . . three hours, that's all it took. And we're still trying to figure it out. What happened? How to respond? What to say? Or perhaps even where to hide . . .

Maybe, there's a chill of fear in the air. Maybe it's not a big thing. But maybe it's like that whisper I felt in the crowded, shoulder to shoulder world, a whisper that says you can't be too careful, better watch your back, keep your head low . . . and ready to flee for your life, from those who seem to have the power of life and death.

Our text this morning shows a side of Elijah we have not seen before: Elijah the fearful.

If there's an injustice, Elijah's not one to watch it on the news; Elijah's on the move, going toe to toe with the powers, not cowering in a cave somewhere.

So that's unusual. But something else, too: Elijah has just come from a spectacular moment in the history of God. Just a chapter ago, on Mount Horeb, Elijah faced down and killed 450 prophets of Baal — these belonged to Elijah's enemy Jezebel. Elijah's God wins hands down. Jezebel, not easily intimidated, sends a warning, not an *assassin*, but a warning that he's next. And Elijah fears and runs for his life.

Now, I can already hear someone saying, what about all that Baal killing? That's not right, we say. I'm with you. Sometimes I listen to Scripture and I just don't get it. We need to see this text for what it is and what it isn't.

Baal worship wasn't something you'd want to bless with ecumenical generosity; it was bloody. But there was blood on everyone's hands, Elijah's included. That means we might struggle to feel much empathy for Elijah. He may have a bounty on his head, but he wasn't guiltless. Let's not "bless" everything that we see in this text, especially its religious violence. At the same time, I don't want us to miss the real burden of the text. This text aims to show how fear gets hold of us sometimes, reducing and distorting our perception of the world God so loves. Look at it again. In chapter nineteen,

Elijah has every reason to be encouraged. A decisive victory on Mt. Carmel is in recent memory or should be. Except today, that's like yesterday's news. Today, Elijah fears. Fears for his life.

And you would think someone so determined to live, would cling to life more. But that's not what happens.

Elijah goes into the wilderness, pulls away from his relationships. Alone, he rested against a broom tree. Not sure of the significance of the tree — Jesus dies on a tree, the cross. Jonah sits beside a broom tree and wishes to die. Maybe it's a giving up place. The text says it was a "*solitary* broom tree" — loneliness is the feeling I get.

The Elijah we see in this text just wasn't himself — the self, robust, the self, whole, the self, richly connected. Elijah wasn't one for surrender, but here we see him surrendering: "Enough," he says. "No more. I'm done." Fear will do that to a person. The text tells us he went to sleep. Maybe it was the kind of sleep he didn't aim to wake up from. Elijah seems almost exhausted unto death. . . .

Ironic that surviving can sometimes feel like dying. Like hiding who you are and who you love can feel like a death repeated every day, without interruption or relief.

But if Elijah flees from life, in the name of fear, God seems restless for life. We see it in three scenes, when God appears, awakening Elijah to something greater than his fear. It doesn't happen all at once. And it's not a spectacular kind of transformation. But it is suggestive of how God enlarges our hearts, though they may be under a cloud of fear.

It takes a while for Elijah to even get that God is stronger than his fears. The third and final exchange between Elijah and God is the most suggestive. But it would be difficult to understand the significance of the text without listening to what Elijah says in response to God's appearing.

Twice Elijah repeats these words, once inside the cave and the next time outside the cave, in the very presence of God: "I have been very zealous for the Lord God Almighty. The Israelites have rejected your covenant, broken down your altars, and put your prophets to death with the sword. I am the only one left and now they are trying to kill me."

He answers this way twice, once *before* he feels God's presence and once *after* he feels God's presence. The text indicates that he heard God, felt God, experienced God. But he didn't really get it. Elijah stood outside the opening of the cave, but maybe his heart was still in that cave. But we should underline one thing in Elijah's favor: even though Elijah doesn't get it, he is moving again. He is talking again. God's future is what gets Elijah moving again. How so? According to Choon-Leong Seow, God answers Elijah's fear with a call to quiet faithfulness, exhibited through ordinary rather than courageous or heroic acts.[5]

Maybe it is God's future that is going to get us moving again. Jesus was hung on a tree, but he didn't stay there. Jesus was buried in a cave, but he didn't stay buried . . . sometimes we forget that, not only about God but also about ourselves.

Maybe this past week, some of us have felt as if fear were gaining the upper hand. Lots of death this week. Perhaps even more fear.

When I saw those open windows at the candlelight vigil, I wasn't seeing everything, or even the most important things. I don't remember who was speaking. Fear guided my eyes as I studied those apartments. And by the way, I'm not judging myself — or anyone else. I saw the walls of a cave, with my fears, real and imagined, projected there. But the beauty of that gathering for me was that God didn't leave me to my fears. I wasn't alone, that was one thing. Behind me, in front of me, beside me — so many people of faith, people who had more to fear than I did, LGBTQ folks, for one, they were there. But even more, I knew it wasn't fear that had gathered us in the first place. It was hope. It was that stirring of God's spirit, that awakened in us a thirst and hunger for justice.

But today, my guess is that all you'll see at the YNot Lot is an empty space. No speakers. No songs. Just an empty space.

Maybe that's where we spend most of our days. Not in a season of spectacular triumphs, but rather pursuing a call to surpassingly ordinary acts in the journey of faith — whose consequence we don't even really fathom.

The Lord told Elijah to go, to return to his way. The Lord didn't say, go find the cure to the cancer of man's inhumanity to man!

The Lord told Elijah go anoint the next king; prepare also for Elisha, your replacement — doesn't sound particularly courageous or historic. We love to chase storms, don't we? We fear them but also film them if we can. But with

---

[5] Choon-Leong Seow, "The First and Second Books of Kings" in *The New Interpreter's Bible*, vol. 3 (Nashville: Abingdon Press, 1999), 143.

God it might be different. God is not in the wind, the earthquake, or the fire. But there, in sheer silence. Thin silence. Silence as fine as sand, we hear God.

It reminds me of something I was told about this church, back in the day when HIV/AIDS was a death sentence. Those with the disease were stigmatized. People literally died alone. Abandoned . . . as the world retreated deep into a cave of fear. I was told about how this church said to those with HIV AIDS — we'll hold you, not only in our prayers, but also in our arms. I don't imagine a news crew showed up to glimpse even one of those exceedingly ordinary, surpassingly precious hugs . . . so ordinary you might not even know what you'd just seen right before your very eyes. If you weren't listening for it, you might miss it altogether. But if you were, maybe it sounded something like Elijah's sheer silence, or the sound of fine sand.

What do you think? You think it was enough to turn a crowd into a congregation; a tomb of sorrows into a sanctuary of courage?

Today, we stand with Orlando on the edge of a mountain, at the edge of mystery; we may not know what's going to happen next. But God has told us to return to the way, to the way of justice, to the way of loving kindness.

I'm not sure what they were doing up in those apartments on Monday. *Probably nothing.* But even if it were something like wind, earthquake, or fire — even if it were something like my worst nightmare, there are so many who love, so many who work for peace, who testify for dignity, who stand with courage.

The Lord is in his holy temple. Let all the world, *and all our fears*, keep silence before him.

May it be so for each us. Amen.

June 19, 2016

Chapter Three

You've Changed

I still dream of catching salmon in Cordova's Copper River in Alaska. I dream of the salmon as they make their return trip to spawn in the waters of their birth. I go to the river of my dreams; throw my line into the water, aiming for the familiar ripple of salmon backs, black and slick, crowding their way up the river; it's as if I can feel the tug of the currents, the anticipation of a salmon striking the spinner.

Odd. It occurred to me the other day that most people in Baltimore don't dream about annual salmon migrations. Part of the "real estate" that forms my identity is as an Alaska Native descendent of the Athabascan people, from my mother's side. Later, as a young person, I lived with my parents (mother and step-father) and siblings in Northern California. We lived at the end of Crooked Mile Court: it was crooked, it was about a mile, and it went down the middle of a steep ravine in the foothills of the Sierra Nevada mountain range. At the time, we enjoyed almost no amenities, including electricity or water. We lived in what we fondly called our "Bisqueen Shack" — a framed out building, half enclosed with plywood and half-sealed by thick sheets of semi-translucent plastic. This was an improvement over the trailer we had lived in before. We took showers outdoors, near the well; for the longest time, we had no hot water. I hated showers. We also watched as this community changed from a place where the rural poor could live to a community dominated by middle class and upper middle-class residents — not only did they drive up the property values, they also drove the cultural values. I aspired to those values and resented them. Culturally, my roots were mixed (and likewise conflicted): Native on my mother's side and on my step-dad's side (with whom I grew up), white Midwestern.

Now, I often wonder, will I ever return home? What is home for me? The rivers that I dream about — will I ever fish those waters again? Probably not. And even if I could return, would it be home anymore?

Home is not just a matter of real estate; it has to do with worldview. Or who you love. Or by whom you are loved. That's the story I sense in the Book of Ruth. Naomi experiences a massive upheaval in her worldview through the agency of Ruth, a Moabite who "clings" to her as a husband would cling to his wife. She defies all the ordinary conventions of gender construction, not only famously (or infamously) with Boaz on the threshing floor, but especially with Naomi, on the road back home to Bethlehem.

Ruth impresses me as a Christ figure, clinging to us with a scandalous love. That love changes us and, in some ways, makes it impossible for us to return to the worldviews that we may have taken for granted before. Maybe that's what Paul means when he declares that in Christ there is neither Jew nor Gentile, male nor female, slave nor free. These identities are too small, too parochial for the new creation in Christ.

When I imagine Naomi, I know I am thinking of myself, but especially, of my mother, who today lives in the urban sprawl of Sacramento, California. We talk sometimes about going home. She says Alaska's not her home anymore. Still, she reads the online version of the *Cordova Times*. Maybe I was thinking of my mom, and probably myself, when I tried to imagine Naomi's internal conflict: "She's looking for an address to park the heart that she's got, but she doesn't realize that her heart has changed. . . ."

Sermon

> *"Do not press me to leave you*
> *or to turn back from following you!*
> *Where you go, I will go;*
> *where you lodge,*
> *I will lodge; your people shall be my people,*
> *and your God my God.*
> *Where you die, I will die —*
> *there will I be buried.*
> *May the Lord do thus and so to me,*
> *and more as well,*
> *if even death parts me from you!"*
>
> *So Naomi returned together with Ruth the Moabite, her daughter-in-law, who came back with her from the country of Moab. They came to Bethlehem at the beginning of the barley harvest.*
>
> —Ruth 1:16b-17; 22

Ruth's narrator paints a picture that looks almost like a biblical version of the American dream — except for some ominous details that surface along the way. Naomi, her name means Sweetness of the Lord, marries Elimelech, whose name means, God Reigns. Lovely couple. So much promise. Her cheeks radiate youth and joy. And Elimelech . . . it's the only time we ever meet him in the Bible, but he sounds like a fine young man. But perhaps he didn't come from money. After all, famine struck and not everyone left Bethlehem, but Elimelech did. Maybe he was a country boy, and you know how it is with country boys, they can survive. . . . And when famine came, our country boy aimed on surviving. Told Sweetness of the Lord Naomi, "Pack up the boys! Get the camel ready — we're goin' to Moab!"

And she went, because, you know, that was what she was supposed to do as the good wife, as a good mother. But things fall apart. First, they left home. *That* was an adjustment. But then the boys married a couple of Moabite girls, Ruth and Orpah. *That* wasn't what Naomi had in mind. Moabites. Ruth's narrator doesn't want us to miss this piece of the story. They went to Moab. They married Moabite women. Almost every time the narrator mentions Ruth, she writes, "Ruth the Moabite" . . . there was some bad blood between Israel and Moab, went back generations.

"But, okay," says our Naomi. "I want to see our boys happy, married off, with their own kids. And anyway, they seem like nice enough girls."

Adapt. Adjust. Compromise. Such is life. You don't get to choose your in-laws — they get chosen for you!

But then Elimelech, our country boy who survives — well, one day he didn't. And then her two sons also die. Childless. And then, by verse five, Naomi is no longer a wife, or a mother to her two sons, or a member of a larger community.

"Only the woman was left," says our narrator. According to Phyllis Trible, a feminist scholar, Naomi stands alone. Not the Sweetness of the Lord. Not the wife of Elimelech. Not the mother to her sons. Only the woman was left — without companion, without vocation, without human or, perhaps, even divine relation. None of the tender ties of family were left to her.[6] Then verse six: "She started to return with her daughters-in-law from the country of Moab, for she had heard rumors, talk that the Lord had considered his people and given them food."

Return. Go back. Turn around. The Hebrew word, *shub* appears fifteen times in Ruth and twelve times in chapter one alone.[7] That means we probably need to pay attention. It suggests a physical journey. It also connotes a form of religious repentance or returning to the worship of God. Some view this story through the latter idea, that what we are seeing here is a form of "repentance" — Naomi's repentance from the culture of Moab, the sense that Israel's God is better than Moab's god and so on. There's some of that to be sure, but I

---

[6] Phyllis Trible, *God and the Rhetoric of Sexuality* (Philadelphia: Fortress Press, 1978), 167.
[7] Kathleen A. Robertson Farmer, "The Book of Ruth" in *The New Interpreter's Bible*, vol. 2 (Nashville: Abingdon Press, 1998), 899.

wouldn't want to lose the physical journey or the vexing problem of worldview that appears to be at the heart of this text. Trible suggests that Naomi is not only returning to a country, but she is also trying to return to a worldview that no longer works. And she wants her daughters-in-law to do the same. At least three times she tells them, go back/turn back:

- To your mother's house (8);

- Turn back to your nation, why would you go with me (11);

- Return . . . go your way (12).

This command "go back" includes not only Naomi, but her daughters-in-law. Naomi intends a physical return but also a return or "going back" to the worldview that let her down.[8]

On first glance, this seems silly. Why would you go back to something that was so flawed? Easy for us to say, but if it's the only world you've ever known, and it gets taken from you, maybe a part of you just wants to get it back, even if it was flawed to begin with. Do you think that's a possibility?

I was in my late twenties and was visiting my mom in California. I'd moved away by then. Gone to graduate school and started my grownup life. But I was back home visiting for a couple of weeks. And we were literally driving down memory lane, Crooked Mile Court, driving through the neighborhood where I spent my teenage years. We reminisced about our walks, how we used to cut through old Vincinni's property, slipping between barbed wire, ignoring the "no trespass" signs to get to our favorite swimming hole on the American River; we drove by the house we called home as kids; we wondered whatever happened to Jimmy Norris (didn't he join the Navy?), or his little sister Krissy (where did she end up?), or John Lamagno (I heard that he was killed in a motorcycle crash) . . . and so it went. And then, as we rounded a corner, my mom said, "You won't be able to come back here. . . ."

"What do you mean I can't come back here?" I shot back. "I can come back here anytime I want! I could live here if I wanted —"

"No, that's not what I mean," she said. "You can live here, live wherever you want. That's not what I'm saying. I'm saying you can't go back to be the person you were. You have changed."

---

[8] Trible, *God and the Rhetoric of Sexuality*, 170-1.

I thought about that for a long time. I'm still thinking about it! I was looking for real estate, but she was talking about a worldview.

And maybe something like that has happened with Naomi. But she doesn't really recognize it yet. She's looking for an address to park the heart that she's got but she doesn't realize that her heart has changed, and maybe the old worldview won't hold everything she has become, everyone she has loved, and all that she has lost in love. She thinks she's returning to a street address, where she can park her life, but in fact, the return we see unfolding in her life is a profound one. Even if all she wanted was a street address, too much has happened . . . this will not be an easy return. You see there's an *eruption* or *disruption* or *interruption* in Naomi's worldview and it appears, interestingly enough in the second half of verse 8: "May the Lord deal kindly with you . . ."

This is where Naomi is telling her daughters-in-law to go home, that they were about to part ways, finally and forever, and what she appears to give them is a traditional blessing, a juiced-up version of "God bless your heart!" That's what it looks like, but the gospel is in the details. And the detail we have in front of us is actually a problem, namely a grammatical corruption in the Hebrew.

The verb, "to give" (translated in the NRSV as "to deal") is missing its object. The sentence breaks right after Naomi says, "May the Lord give. . . ." We're waiting for the object of the verb: Gives what? Gives misery? Gives nothing?

Most translations smooth out the syntax, supplying an object to the verb. This is a religious formula, something like, "bless your heart." Only in this case the object is missing. So here, the expected thing that God would *give* is kindness, mercy, or full reward. That's how the NRSV solves the problem. Others look to verse nine, believing that the object got stuck in traffic — so it shows up late. So the sentence would be, "May the Lord . . . give you security in your husband's house." Sounds strained to me.

I like the suggestion of Jeremy Schipper, Old Testament scholar and good friend of mine from Ph.D. days. Jeremy wonders if the sentence is intentional the way it is, as if Naomi began by offering this formulaic blessing, "May the Lord give you his kindness . . ." but her voice broke, her words faltered, just as her worldview had faltered.

"May the Lord give to you . . . *oh forget it!*"⁹

"I can't do this anymore. Good luck to you girls. You've been so good to me. I'm sorry it turned out like this. Maybe you'll have better luck with your gods than I have had with my God."

That has the ring of truth to me. How about you? I feel the exhaustion in my bones, even if I don't always get the grammar. I get the hurt. God's kindness to her seems in short supply. *There's a gulf between the word of faith she speaks and the world of hurt she feels.* Even so, she urges her daughters-in-law to return to the very world that caused the hurt. Initially, both Ruth and Orpah refuse. The bond they feel is real. But so also is the pull to go back to the way things were, even if they weren't ideal. Ultimately, Orpah goes back . . . just as Naomi tries to go back. The text underlines the difference between the two daughters: they all wept together. Orpah kissed her mother-in-law, but Ruth clung to her. And apparently wouldn't let go.

The verb here, clung, is used in Genesis when God says a man shall cling to a woman, his wife. This is a vow, not unlike a marriage vow, so this should give us pause.[10]

In the ancient world where women were supposed to cling to men for their survival, for their economic security, Ruth clinging to Naomi seems very much out of the ordinary. Ruth declares a love without interruption, a faithfulness without shadow: Where you go, I will go. The Hebrew makes it even more staggering . . . there is no "to be" verb in the Hebrew:

Where you go, I go;
Where you lodge, I lodge;
Your people; my people;
Your God; my God;
Your death; my death;
Your tomb; my tomb.[11]

As if, in some profound way, the world inhabited by Naomi has been enlarged by unlikely, improbable, even scandalous love — love too large for the status quo, love too mysterious for the Supreme Court; love too unruly for seminary; too fearless for the fearful; love too much even for Naomi to

---

[9] Jeremy Schipper, *Ruth: A New Translation with Introduction and Commentary* in The Anchor Yale Bible Series (New Haven: Yale University Press, 2016), 93.
[10] Robertson Farmer, "The Book of Ruth" in *New Interpreter's Bible*, 905.
[11] Adapted from Schipper, *Ruth: A New Translation*, 100.

really understand. A love that would not let Naomi go back . . . to the way things were or even let her remain in the bitterness she was feeling.

And Naomi, seeing that Ruth will not turn back . . . seeing this, she says nothing more to her. I don't know what that silence means to you. But I guess if someone said to me what Ruth said to Naomi, I'd need to think about that for a very, very, very, very long time. Naomi starts back, on the return trip, and maybe she thinks she's looking for real estate, but she's changed, whether she knows it or not — she's been touched by a worldview expanding with God's love and that's a world expanding at the speed of light.

Our street address here at First and Franklin is 210 West Madison Street. You can come back here anytime. But you know, if you leave this place, I hope you will hear somehow, somewhere, from someone an improbable word of love. Maybe you will hear the echo of Ruth's voice in Christ's voice at this table:

> Take, this my body. Eat.

> Take, this my blood. Drink.

A vow like that will rock your world. It may make you ask questions you'd never asked before.

You may leave this place pondering rather than talking. Go back to your house, your tribe, your people . . . go back to the house you call home, to the circle of people you call friends . . . but reflect, if you can, on this unusual love, a love that will not let you go . . . unchanged, untouched, unloved. You've changed. May it be so for each of us. Amen.

July 3, 2016

Chapter Four

By Chance It Happened

Some theologians harbor deep suspicions towards biblical scholars. I don't share their suspicions — I figure if I'm given a valley of dry bones (i.e. rather dry essays and commentary by biblical scholars) to wander around in, so be it. God has done more with less. But I do get the issue. While it is not true across the board, there is a particular class of scholar that shows an incredible arrogance towards the text, writing as if whoever penned the "muddled syntax" in question was a ninny. According to them, any idiot could do better. In their scholarly judgment (which is always considered, exhaustively footnoted, and cross-referenced) biblical writers get their geography wrong, their history garbled, their facts confused, and their ideologically driven assertions are dubious if not outright fabrications. They can look at a text, especially its theological trappings, with the zeal of the original iconoclast, ripping out thick locks of pious belief, mercilessly dismissing the theological interpretations of Christian tradition as implausible at best and corrupt at worst.

Often hard to hear as people of faith — and not much prettier to read as a pastoral theologian. But it is especially difficult when the biblical scholar in question is a good friend of yours, as is the case with Jeremy Schipper. His commentary on Ruth was especially influential for me. Back in seminary, I felt a kind of rebel solidarity with this quirky, intelligent Ph.D. student in Old Testament studies. Today, Jeremy is a mature biblical scholar, respected by his guild. I still count him as a friend, though we haven't visited in a long time.

In a sense, as I opened his book on Ruth, I felt like we were about ready to get together again, just as we did at Princeton. With that sense of anticipation, I found a comfortable spot with his thin but substantial contribution to Ruth scholarship. I dug in. And the more I read, the more concerned I became. As I digested what seemed like a heartless dismissal of traditional readings of Ruth (e.g. that God's hand moved invisibly in the text, providing a providential plan for Naomi's future), I grieved. I wanted to argue with him: "Jeremy, you can't simply erase God from the picture here! You need to read the text canonically, in the broad sweep of the biblical story. Okay, so God doesn't speak in this text, doesn't even act in an especially pronounced way, but it's in the context of canon, where God speaks, and acts, and intervenes. So what if you don't see God actively manipulating the story? Haven't you heard of Adam Smith's invisible hand? If capitalism has an invisible hand, surely God does too! Are you going to reduce this love story to a story of chance encounters and chance redemption?"

But Jeremy's my friend. While I disagreed with him in places or felt that he overstated his case in others, I had to admit that he had produced a fine and compelling piece of biblical scholarship on the Book of Ruth. And more than that: perhaps, after all, I had not given Ruth a full hearing. I said to myself, "Maybe he's right. Maybe there's something that I am missing if I go to God's providential design too soon. Chance, eh?"

You will see that, in the end, I was not quite willing to surrender providence . . . but I thought at least I would give Jeremy a chance . . . and perhaps Ruth, too!

Sermon

> *And Ruth the Moabite said to Naomi, "Let me go to the field and glean among the ears of the grain, behind someone in whose sight I may find favor." She said to her, "Go my daughter." So she went. She came and gleaned in the field behind the reapers. As it happened, she came to the part of the field belonging to Boaz, who was of the family of Elimelech. Just then Boaz came from Bethlehem.*
>
> — Ruth 1:22b-2:23

It happened by chance. A literal, wooden translation of the text says that Ruth's chance chanced upon the field belonging to Boaz.[12] Ruth, finding herself a stranger in a strange land, appears to roll the dice of fate, throwing her destiny into the possibility rather than the promise of a merciful world . . . and if we're honest, the odds seem to be stacked against her . . . and if they are against her, perhaps they are also against us. Never mind the odds, says our Ruth. Maybe it was her youth, maybe it was just necessity itself . . . but she went armed with little more than the chance that she might find security, that she might know the possibility of a future.

"Let me go out to the fields," she says to her mother-in-law, "to harvest what the harvesters leave behind . . . perhaps someone will notice me." By chance, that someone turned out to be Boaz. Naomi, for whom chance has been cruel, says only, "Go my daughter." Some interpreters make this out as a term of endearment, that perhaps we're seeing a thaw in Naomi. After all she says, "my daughter." That's something. But notice what she does not say. She does

---

[12] Schipper, *Ruth: A New Translation*, 117.

not say, *God go with you, my daughter.* Not even good luck, my child. Simply "Go" ... without blessing; go without encouragement; go even into harm's way without warning. We can appreciate how Naomi might have felt — rolling the dice had not been kind to her. Or maybe *God* had not been kind to her. Either way, she went away full but she had returned empty.

Go, she said. Just go. Maybe part of Naomi's bitterness was amplified by this stray daughter-in-law, a bit like a stray cat, a stray that no one wants to claim — and yet it wraps itself around your leg, a perfect stranger, and it stays with you, and you can't shake it off. It's a stranger, but it clings to you as if you were long lost friends.

Maybe Naomi's "go" is a firm, if not cruel, shaking off of this stray cat, this Moabite girl, this chance relation.

Chance is unfamiliar territory for people of faith, especially when reading Scripture. Chance is fine for winning the lottery; not so much for God. In church, we read Scripture with an eye out for God. Chance belongs to a different department. That means the traditional reading of Ruth is that God is working, like a computer program that runs behind the screen, as you work. It's running but you don't see it. So, in Ruth, we are to see God as the "invisible" actor, the "unseen" agent of the action in the story. This is the way we are accustomed to reading the text, and God in the text, Ruth included. Good enough. Still, if we try to insert God into every page, into every gesture, we lose something of this text. What if we give a chance to chance this morning?

If we choose the lens of chance rather than providence, we see things we might have missed. For instance, one writer believes that Ruth is the female counter-part to Abraham — like Abraham, she leaves her country, becomes a stranger in a strange land. However, there is at least one significant difference between Abraham and Ruth: Abraham goes to that strange land because God commands him to go: "Go to the land that I will show you." Ruth acts on no such command. She initiates. She chooses. She speaks. She questions.[13]

Our narrator does not report that God woke Boaz up in a dream, like he woke up Joseph and told him what to do with a certain young woman by the name of Mary, mother of Jesus ... to the contrary, in Ruth, a woman (not God!) wakes up Boaz from a beer induced slumber, wakes him up in more

---

[13] Kirsten Nielsen, *Ruth: A Commentary*, James L. Mays, eds., et. al. (Louisville: Westminster John Knox Press, 1997, 49.

ways than one — Jason Kissel, our music minister, suggests we call next week's sermon, *Hot and Saucy*!

In just two places, the narrator explicitly assigns an act of mercy to God: the first time happens in chapter 1 verse 6, God gives fertility to the land, and in the fourth chapter, verse 13, God gives conception to the womb. The fertility of the land and womb were things the ancient world believed were solely God's area of expertise. Otherwise, the narrator leaves much to chance or human agency. . . whether or not Boaz will "notice" Ruth; or whether a good time on the threshing floor will turn into anything more than a good time on the threshing floor.[14]

Even the thing that seems to guarantee a happy outcome for Ruth and Naomi, that Boaz is a close relation to Naomi's dead husband, Elimelech, isn't such a sure thing. This, by the way, is a piece of Old Testament law which said if a husband should die, his brother (or close male relative) was obligated to marry his widow, so that the family name could go on. So, Naomi hopes this might be the outcome of Ruth's encounter with Boaz in the field.

It's the law, so perhaps there's not so much chance as you'd expect. Maybe, maybe not. Why the ambiguity? To begin with, if it were such a sure thing that the law would protect Naomi, the book would have ended at chapter one. Naomi would have run straight to her redeemer's house and demanded that he fulfill his legal obligation to her, as the widow of Elimelech. End of story. But of course, she doesn't do this; perhaps she knew the way the law was applied — differently to some than to others. Additionally, it will also turn out that Boaz is not even the nearest kin to Elimelech, that there is someone else. The narrator deliberately undermines any "legal" certainty concerning the fate of Naomi.

We just don't know. Which, as it happens, feels a lot like the life we live on most days: will love grow or will love perish? Will success be ours or will it belong to someone else? I was talking to a friend the other night about a corporate merger that took place in a company he had worked for: "We were on the losing end," he said. "It became pretty clear that in the new configuration, our division was on its way out. It all depends on whose company policies win — if it's yours, you've got a chance, but if not, well, there's not much you can do. . . ."

A luck of the draw. And yet only *somewhat* analogous to what we see in Ruth. Somewhat because it seems that some of us "feel" exposed to chance more

---

[14] Schipper, *Ruth: A New Translation*, 29-35.

than others. Take Maria for example. Maria was an undocumented migrant from Mexico. I met her in Tucson, Arizona, where I was doing research for a book I was working on at the time.[15] She told her story, how she narrowly avoided arrest by hiding inside a culvert, while U.S. Border Patrol helicopters circled overhead, and police dogs searched on the ground down below. As she spoke, she mimed the story with her body, how it was in the culvert, how she looked up through the bramble into the sky, hoping to see and yet remain unseen. She told how it was when the coyote, the human smuggler, started going in circles in the desert. She thinks he was high. She managed to escape the desert but not trouble. Only a couple of days before we talked, she had collapsed, unconscious, exhausted in a convenience store in a town not far from Tucson. Chance so close, so terrifying it shapes your body, the way you tell the story.

I wonder what Maria would have thought of Ruth. Would she recognize the danger of exposure, the possibility of sexual assault, the enormous risks shouldered by the poor as they take a chance at gaining security, achieving economic stability? Would she recognize Ruth's theology? A theology which comes from low down, on the ground, in the field during the harvest season; or on the threshing floor, late at night; or perhaps from a hiding place in a culvert — a place that seems more random than providential. She might also question this text. Chance can be cruel. One gets lucky; the other does not. If one escapes assault, the other is its victim. One perishes; another survives. Chance is a mixed bag at best.

Then we meet Boaz, the owner of the field. The narrator paints Boaz as a "mighty man" and his name sounds like the Hebrew word for pillar, so maybe his name would be better translated as Pillar of the Village.

Ruth happens to glean in his field; Boaz happens to notice Ruth. That chance evolves into recognition, notice. Initially Boaz doesn't talk *to* Ruth but *about* her. He talks to one of his head field hands and asks, "Who is this girl?" He shrugs, "She's the Moabite that came with Naomi."

"Ah yes," he says. "Now I remember . . . so *this* is Ruth." Then, without explanation, the field hand drops out of the picture. The distance between Boaz and Ruth disappears. Boaz speaks directly to Ruth and Ruth directly to Boaz. Boaz tells her to "stay close" or "cling" to his field, using the same verb used by the narrator to describe Ruth's determination to stay with Naomi.[16] And she asks, "Why have you noticed me, why of all of these have you seen

---

[15] See Robert P. Hoch, *By the Rivers of Babylon: Blueprint for a Church in Exile* (Minneapolis: Fortress Press, 2014).
[16] Robertson Farmer, "The Book of Ruth" in *The New Interpreter's Bible*, 917.

me, noticed me, a stranger in your midst?" Good question, Ruth. Inquiring minds would like to know! Is it the flesh quickened by physical desire that got Ruth noticed or was it the sense of sober moral obligation that Boaz feels towards her that led him to "notice" the Moabite woman?

Well, we don't know. We have theories. We have ideas. But we don't know. All we know is that a passing glance at a field of anonymous laborers had turned into something else . . . this playful, curiously intimate banter between erstwhile strangers.

She asks Boaz, "Why did you see me, a stranger, why do your eyes linger with me, one among many, why do you speak to me, a woman and a foreigner?" Maybe Ruth was teasing Boaz, playfully questioning the motives of this pillar of society? Possibly. But her question also suggests that something has changed this chance meeting into something stronger, something more likely to probe our commitments, to test our convictions.

And Ruth doesn't waste time. When Boaz gets all religious on her — "May the Lord reward you for your deeds, may the Lord shelter you under her wings!" — Ruth's says, "May I continue to find favor in *your* sight, my lord, for *you* have comforted me. . . ." Boaz commends Ruth's future well-being to God; but Ruth's response underscores the human side of mercy.

Now some of us may be objecting to the worldview here — women depending on men for their security is one. Or perhaps to the heterosexual norms being superimposed by this text. Objections granted! With Ruth, the human side of mercy reflects the cultural assumptions of the biblical period — that a woman's security came primarily from two things, children, specifically sons, and their husbands. We can understand this without blessing its cultural trappings — if we can do that, we may still discover wisdom here.

What wisdom? The rest of the story tells how Boaz went beyond the legal obligation that he had to the poor. Way beyond. At the end of the day, she walks away with between 30 and 50 pounds of grain — not a bad haul for a day of begging. And Ruth, of course, is supposed to think this is all perfectly natural; that this is the way things happen all the time in Bethlehem. Charm city indeed! And then Naomi comes back into the story . . . we haven't seen or heard from her since verse two. The verb "to see" returns — Naomi "saw" how much Ruth had gleaned; and maybe something in her heart quickened. It seemed like chance . . . but was it? Was it really? At what point does chance turn into providence?

You may wonder about how I "happened" to have my conversation with Maria in Tucson. Mostly, the Marias of this world work in the field or in the kitchen — but this Maria stood out, not so much because she was different from all the other Marias but because by chance someone had noticed, someone had cared enough to think about, to consider the welfare of people like her. By chance, this Maria collapsed in a convenience store and not in the desert. By chance, a nurse from a church with a ministry to migrants was called to get her the medical care she needed; by chance she was driven to the shelter at Casa Mariposa, the Butterfly House, a temporary sanctuary for undocumented immigrants. By chance, she was willing to talk with me, a stranger, to tell her story. By chance, I remember how she sat on the couch across from me, wearing a faded orange t-shirt, her legs curled up beneath her.

By chance, by chance . . . it seemed like chance . . . but it felt like providence. Or at least the beginning of something like providence. At the end of chapter two, Ruth returns to live with her mother-in-law. The harvest was over. Boaz had gone back to his big house. Ruth and Naomi had gone back to their shack of poverty. Their future still uncertain.

Chance, it seems, will only go so far.

July 10, 2016

Chapter Five

What Happens in Vegas . . .

If you never preached from the Book of Ruth, you would never have the opportunity to suggest that worship on a Sunday morning was little more than a religious roll in the hay. This is something for which preachers might be grateful. But our worshippers might feel deprived of — how shall we say it? — a good time.

Sorry. But you understand my predicament, no? The narrator's wordplay in chapter three is suggestive, the euphemisms of "knowing" and "uncovering" and "exposing" carry their well-known associations, even without knowledge of biblical Hebrew. And I think we might spend twenty minutes on a Sunday morning deciphering just what happened between Ruth and Boaz on the threshing floor. But even more scandalous, and probably more apt for our reading of Ruth, is the idea that the church bathes itself in a spirituality that has about as much lasting power as a night on the threshing floor, the biblical equivalent of a one-night stand. And yet, when the church gropes for the holy, we discover more than a divine being, but a personal Lord who commands our obedience in the light of day.

I enjoyed preaching this sermon. Part of it goes to the freedom (and, yes, mischief) of the analogy. In this case, the analogy of the threshing floor finds its way, almost effortlessly, to the "threshing floor" of congregational life, where we seek to know God and be known by God but are perhaps less willing to carry the promises we make beyond the noon hour. We grope for the selfish gratification of prayer and praise but seem almost indifferent to the ethical command implied by the One to whom we pray; we make theological love on top of a comforting grain heap of religious security but seldom awaken with a specific name on our lips, an obligation to be in covenant relationship with the least of these.

Admittedly, my reading of Ruth's threshing floor was more ecclesiological than the writer intended. But that's the beauty of an analogy: it comes to us as an imaginative rather than prescriptive engagement with the text. In this way, perhaps, we meet Christ in Ruth. As John records, we would see Jesus. Boaz saw not only a woman, but eventually Ruth, one whose command he obeyed. Boaz leaves that threshing floor with more than an empty promise — he goes out to "settle the matter" that has been broached in the whispered context of physical intimacy. The sermon ends by recalling that we perhaps have experienced some presence, some encounter which we cannot simply leave at the threshing floor of the numinous experience. And perhaps the threshing floor isn't beyond redemption; perhaps it is the very site of our redemption in Christ. Just as we claim God in our prayers, so God claims us in our lives — on the threshing floor and beyond.

Sermon

> *When Boaz had eaten and drunk, and he was in a contented mood, he went to lie down at the end of the heap of grain. Then she came stealthily and uncovered his feet, and lay down. At midnight the man was startled, and turned over, and there, lying at his feet, was a woman! He said, "Who are you?" And she answered, "I am Ruth, your servant; spread your cloak over your servant, for you are next-of-kin."*
>
> — Ruth 3:8-9

The stakes of Naomi's match-making gamble are high ... some would say too high to seriously entertain.

It's certainly risky, if not for Naomi (who doesn't seem to have much to lose) then surely for Ruth. What could go wrong? Well, it seems like virtually everything could go wrong, but especially risky is the culture of the threshing floor itself. Indeed, after my exhaustive reading of this text, I have concluded that meeting at the threshing floor was code, code for what the world has agreed not to remember.

In truth, it's actually code for a little lake I knew about as a kid. Arrowbee Lake, a great place for taking a dip on a hot summer afternoon ... but later, when I became a teen, it turned out it was another place altogether, especially late at night. At night, it became a place of mysteries, mysteries of moonlit skin, moist lips, and deliciously sensuous waters ... there might have been promises, there might have been prayers, and maybe even one or two of them were answered (I won't tell you which!) — but as in Vegas, what happened there stayed there! This reminds me of church. Excuse me? What did you say? Vegas? Arrowbee Lake? A threshing floor? How's that? Well, hear me out — and maybe you'll agree or maybe not, but it's hard to resist a comparison with this "threshing floor" — the threshing floor we call the church at worship.

Is this thing we're doing here, is it a religious roll in the hay? Is this our secret place, known only to the initiated, where we can meet, our souls exposed, our dark places lit in ways we don't understand but we definitely enjoy? Are our prayers — are they more flirtatious than faithful? Is church code for our deepest thirsts and yet at the same time the place where we hold to an unspoken agreement that what happens here stays here? As we bathe in the shadows of the holy, as we pray with sighs too deep for words, as we groan in the arms of the holy, as we savor the answered prayer — is it a bit like that? Like we don't really imagine anything taking hold here, past the hour, beyond the day?

Who can blame us, really? I'm told that those with low expectations are happier than the folks with high expectations. And maybe it's true.

You pray for peace, but what do you really expect from that prayer? Feels good to say it maybe. And maybe in the mysterious calculus of the cosmos, saying such things makes a difference. But the truth is your day won't come to a grinding, outraged halt if peace on earth does not come today, or tomorrow, or even in your lifetime. Your heart, my heart aches for human kindness, but really, do you think singing a hymn is going to get you any closer to loving your enemy?

I don't want to sound harsh or cynical. I honestly don't think we're looking for cheap thrills (except for when we are). Mostly, I wonder if the things we grope for under cover of this holy night, perhaps these things are beyond our attaining, beyond our keeping . . . too big for mere mortals. Peace. Reconciliation. Love. Salvation. So we lower our expectations a notch . . . from heavenly promises to the level of the threshing floor.

Perhaps today's text challenges us in this way, not necessarily to avoid the threshing floor, but never be reduced to it, to never be seduced by its spirit.

At the start, this text sounds like the clichéd Harlequin style seduction scene. Naomi tells Ruth to get out that sexy little number she's got in the closet (you know the one?); anoint herself with perfume, maybe something like Chance by Chanel; wait until Boaz has eaten and is in a "contented mood" — then go to him and, according to Naomi, the man will tell you what to do.

Feminist scholars believe that Naomi's advice reflects a sexual culture dominated by what men want from women. So glad we've gotten over that, aren't you! In any event, Naomi tells Ruth that Boaz will lead in the encounter.

Ruth's role, according to Naomi, is passive: follow his instructions. And the text says that Ruth did all that Naomi told her.

Except she didn't, at least not exactly.

Before we talk about what Ruth did (or didn't do), it might be well to take a closer look at the threshing floor scene. No one knows precisely what happened on the threshing floor. But the language is suggestive. According to one commentator, terms that carry sexual overtones occur "frequently and repeatedly throughout Ruth 3" — including the verb, "to know" (five times); "to lie down" (eight times); "to undress" (two times); "to enter" (seven times); plus, euphemistic terms like "feet" and the language about spreading Boaz's cloak over Ruth. None of this proves what happened between Ruth and Boaz, but we can safely conclude that whatever it was, it was more involved than a platonic chat.[17]

Okay. So the verbs imply what they imply. Consensus here. However, an interesting debate arises around one critical verb, to expose or to uncover — who did Ruth expose? Did Ruth expose Boaz or did Ruth expose herself? Most translations have Ruth "uncovering" Boaz's toes. This is a euphemism for "exposing" Boaz's "family jewels" (another euphemism), but other scholars wonder if, in fact, a better translation would have Ruth exposing herself to Boaz. Why the difference of opinion? One camp says that Ruth taking the initiative in this scene is what's intended — that's how we've experienced Ruth. Irrespective of Naomi's advice, Ruth does and says precisely what Ruth does and says. Ruth clings, Orpah leaves; Ruth vows her faithfulness; Naomi resigns her hope. Ruth stands out for initiative, for the unexpected action, maybe even the unprecedented action.[18]

Which do you prefer? Either way, it's pretty risqué stuff for a Sunday morning. I'll leave that conversation for the drive home with the kids.

But I am struck by all this exposure going on . . . which, strangely enough, brings to mind the first words in John Calvin's *The Institutes of the Christian Religion*, the theological Bible of the Presbyterian Church. He writes, "The beginning of true and substantial wisdom is the knowledge of God and the knowledge of humankind, but which comes first, the knowledge of God or the knowledge of the human being, we cannot tell."

Perhaps this text suggests to us the moment when we realize that we are known by God . . . and that, just as unsettling, we may have glimpsed a bit of God's glory with our own eyes.

When this happens in the Bible, when people see God's glory, there's more than a little after-glow. Paul is struck blind. After gazing on God, Moses' face

---

[17] Schipper, *Ruth: A New Translation*, 156-157.
[18] Nielsen, *Ruth: A Commentary*, 69.

was so bright, the people could not bear to look at him. He had to wear a veil to diminish the after-glow of glory. And maybe we get a sense of the double action of exposure in the story of Jesus in John's gospel. This is the gospel quoted in this pulpit: "Sir, we would see Jesus." We would see light. We would see God, the Word made flesh.

And in seeing the flesh of the Word, we see glory, but we recognize Jesus. Boaz *saw* a woman, but he *recognized* Ruth.

In today's text, just before Ruth came to the threshing floor, Boaz was in a contented mood. He'd had a few. The grain was heaped up in great piles of economic surplus. But in a moment, all that contentedness would be upset. Boaz was startled by what he saw: A woman! That's enough. He saw more than he expected to see. But then Ruth doesn't leave it there. She says to him, "I am Ruth, your maidservant. Spread your cloak over me, for I am your next of kin" (9). This was equivalent to saying, "You, Boaz, are to serve as our redeemer." This is not charity — nor is this the language of the threshing floor — but rather it is the language of covenant, of promise, of obligation. And Boaz responds positively, mostly. First, he says, Yes, it is true what you say, I am a near kinsman (the first time that he actually admits to being her redeemer) but then he says, I'm not the *nearest* of kin. There's someone closer than I am.

Well, the truth is, not only is Boaz unsettled, *things leading to redemption* are not settled. Boaz turns over, startled, and now finds himself face to face with Ruth, who leads the narrative with a claim, a claim on his actions. *Not, what are you willing to promise, but what kind of fruit will your promise produce?* We get the sense that with the book of Ruth, words and actions matter. Words do not vanish just because they are spoken on the threshing floor. Words like redemption awaken the morally acquiescent to undertake action, deeds.[19]

Don't listen to what love says, attend to what love does. Maybe that's *part* of the word to us today. I say part because *what* love says and *how* it says it belong together. I don't want to lose that. If we lose the "how" we might as well get rid of Ruth, which is at least a beautiful work of literary art. Of course, if it stays there, if the love we pray about never does what it says, then we probably ought not trust it.

At the end of today's chapter, after hearing all that Boaz had done, Naomi tells Ruth that he will not rest until the matter is settled.

---

[19] Schipper, *Ruth: A New Translation*, 28.

Like peace. Like reconciliation. Like love. Like safe streets. It's a matter to be settled, isn't it? Or is it just talk?

Ask Dominic Nell what he thinks. A resident of Sandtown-Winchester, he saw kids playing with toy guns, and it bothered him. "[The kids kept saying], 'pow, pow, pow!' Everybody's killing everybody, the police just killed somebody on TV!'" Dominic works as a photographer and so he asked if the boys would like to "shoot" pictures with his camera instead. One asked, "Can you put real bullets in it?"

Sounds like these boys are being formed by the mentality of the killing fields — what do you think?

Dominic could have left it at that, shrugged his shoulders, shook his head. Others feel the same way. A toy gun manufacturer says the guns aren't the problem — it's the mentality of our world. We've gone mad, he says. But Dominic did more than shake his head. He did something. "In the heat of everything that's going on," he said, "I wanted to focus on something tangible." He began to visit stores, twenty of them, half of which sold toy guns and, he says, the majority have agreed to stop carrying them.[20] A little thing, to be sure. But he could not rest. And maybe we shouldn't either. After all, we've been startled by God's glory, by God's appearing in Christ. We turned over, intoxicated by religion, only to see the Christ, the lover of our souls.

By the way, if you're not quite ready to have a come to Jesus moment in church today, you're in good company: Boaz doesn't sound exactly love struck. He loads six measures of grain onto Ruth's back. I don't remember too many love stories that include treating your-would-be lover like a beast of burden. Not what I would have expected. But you know, Naomi was right about one thing — old Boaz had some things to figure out. He went out into the neighborhood. Promises made on the threshing floor rose a little higher than the heap of grain, lasted a bit longer than the high or its hangover. He didn't sleep that night or the next day. He was restless in love.

May our prayers rise higher than this grain heap of religious security; may our prayers unsettle this neighborhood with tangible works of mercy. May it not

---

[20] Jesse Coburn, "Grass-Roots Efforts Take Stance Against Toy Guns" in *The Baltimore Sun* (12 July 2016) accessed on May 18, 2018 at
http://www.baltimoresun.com/news/maryland/baltimore-city/bs-md-ci-toy-guns-20160712-story.html.

be said of this church that what happens here, stays here. Seek peace and pursue it, even if it takes as long as we both shall live. Amen.

July 17, 2016

Chapter Six

The Art of the Deal

The campaign and eventual election of Donald Trump was good for Saturday Night Live for the same reason it was challenging for preachers on Sunday morning: for SNL, it was a natural fit, prime opportunity for lampoon and caricature. For preachers who trade on the idea of being pastoral, it created a unique set of challenges: when the powers and principalities act in ways that are grossly unethical, does the pulpit remain silent? I wasn't alone in facing that question. Other pastors were in the same position. I spoke with one respected friend and colleague and he told me that he had people say they weren't coming back because of his preaching. He had been in that pulpit for well-over a decade. In July of 2016, I had been at First & Franklin for one month. I didn't know the congregation. Adjectives that captured something of the place include establishment, quirky, political, LGBTQ, transient (including not only people off the street but also grad students at the nearby universities), rich and poor. A white church and not a white church, at least not in the traditional sense. A city church, in the heart of Baltimore, where we're nearly two-thirds African-American. A bit of establishment, a bit of not-establishment. All these taken together make First & Franklin a diverse congregation. Indeed, on Sundays, our church includes both the housing insecure as well as the real estate wealthy.

It was in this regard that I was also struck by the brazen character of this text, a business deal intruding into what was, ostensibly, a love story. "A man's world [a businessman's world] tells a woman's story," according to Phyllis Trible.[21] We don't think of the gospel revealed in real estate transaction (or an ancient woman's story involving something other than a husband!), but maybe we should. That seems to be at least one upshot of the story of Ruth. Yes, obviously, the story claims more than real estate as its concern, but it is not less than real estate. Churches, of all institutions, should understand that truth. But we spiritualize what Scripture treats concretely.

I located the cut of this text, its claim, in the area of affordable housing. Baltimore, like most cities, subsidizes the wealthy even as it penalizes the poor. We seldom say it aloud, but the true welfare class in the United States is the middle and especially upper, mostly white classes. If they can afford it, middle classes move to the suburbs where they enjoy better funded public schools, cleaner streets, less economic disparity. In downtown Baltimore, the

---

[21] Trible, *God and the Rhetoric of Sexuality*, 166.

very wealthy live in what locals call economic and cultural bubbles (or less charitably, "Disneyland") while within a mile you will find grinding poverty. This isn't an accident. It's social engineering at its worst. It ranges from city councils granting tax abatement to massive corporations — thus starving public schools of needed revenue — to the way lenders systematically excluded entire neighborhoods and small business owned by people of color from lending.

Drive from Darley Park to Harbor East in Baltimore and you will think you have passed through two different countries — and, in a sense, you have. Middle class and wealthy squatters have taken land that once belonged to factory workers, small business owners and so on. It used to be the home of people who were not rich but not poor either. Good paying jobs belonged to African American families. And yet, through gentrification (and the acquiescence of people with power) the squatter class enjoys an ever-greater share of the profits of power but not the social responsibility that comes with it.

Preaching involves personification, that is, giving shape to the voices or experiences suggested by characters within the text. While Naomi had been a prominent figure in previous sermons, I felt like calling out the Boaz of Baltimore in this sermon. His name, Boaz, suggests "mighty pillar" or "strong person". Strong people, people who enjoy the trust of the larger community, have access to power. But if they remain silent, if they don't activate their networks, if they don't pursue a muscular kind of leverage on behalf of the poor in economic and political centers of power, people like Naomi will continue to be exploited. I honestly don't know if Boaz was in the congregation that day. Or if he (she) was, whether they heard their name, their story – or what their story might become.

Sermon

> *No sooner had Boaz gone up to the gate and sat down there than the next-of-kin, of whom Boaz had spoken, came passing by. So Boaz said, "Come over friend; sit down here." And he went over and sat down. Then Boaz took ten men of the elders of the city, and said, "Sit down here"; so they sat down. He then said to the next-of-kin, "Naomi, who has come back from the country of Moab, is selling the parcel of land that belonged to our kinsman Elimelech. So I thought I would tell you of it here, and in the presence of the elders of my people. If you will redeem it, redeem it."*
>
> — Ruth 4:1-4a

If we find gospel in today's text, I suspect it will have something do with real estate. Come to think of it, Donald Trump, real estate mogul and humble nominee of the Grand Old Party, would be pleased with this morning's sermon title. That might be the only thing he likes about today's sermon, but if that's the case, I must be doing something right!

But I don't think *The Donald* will be darkening our door any time soon . . . but if he does, *if he does*, I'd like to make every effort to welcome The Donald. Ushers, if he comes in this morning, a little late maybe 'cause he's busy building walls and skylines, please let him know that the title of today's sermon, *The Art of the Deal*, was inspired by his very own book by that title — it's all about The Donald, isn't it? And who else might inspire a preacher like me?

Well, for one, perhaps today's text. Today's text connects the sale of property or, even more, the profit one might get from property, to the story of God's providential plan. It's almost as if the biblical narrator doubles down on God's promise: You said you were faithful to Abraham, the one to whom you gave property as well as messages of your presence. What evidence of *actual mercy*, the mercy that would be important to someone like Naomi, will you give, O God? We're not talking promises in the sky, but bread in the cupboard; not promises of a place in our father's heavenly house, but a place to call home in this neighborhood, which also happens to be your holy creation.

So, let's see if we can hear gospel in the midst of a real estate transaction. Not usually where we look for gospel, but then again, neither is the threshing floor — and we found it there! So why not in the real estate business?

To begin, was this property mentioned before? No. You didn't miss anything there — but today, in chapter four, Naomi has this piece of property. Isn't she supposed to be poor? It seems like it. That seems to be a contradiction, but it is possible to be land-rich and dirt poor at the same time. "The poor may inherit the earth," says one capitalist, "but they will not get its mineral rights" — true of our world and probably of the ancient world as well. Naomi had land through her husband Elimelech, but when they left to go to the land of Moab, they left (but did not sell) that land behind. The land stood vacant, no improvements being made to it. After ten years or so, maybe it was assumed that they would never come back. Someone began to use the property. Maybe the person was the equivalent of a middle class or even wealthy squatter, using the property but without formally owning it.

Some readers wonder if this person may have been none other than Elimelech's closest male relative, the one who would be obligated to take care of Naomi. The narrator never names this nearest male relative, just calls him a "So and So" and I will too. You know that *So and So*, not quite known but not quite unknown either.[22]

"So and So," they said in the village, "made money off of Naomi's property." You know what I mean? Under-the-table profits, but it was So and So, a respected member of the village, a near relative to Elimelech, so everyone was happy to look the other way, as he made capital improvements to the property.

Until one day, Naomi comes back to the village. Village women don't forget, do they? Neither do real estate agents and their bankers — they may look the other way, but they don't forget. Maybe So and So knows this. As long as no one asks any questions, we'll just pretend that everything is as it should be. Pretend that the poor are poor because they were fated to poverty. That somehow, in their DNA, they carry the genetic sequence of poverty. Born for rags and destined to die in them. Just as we were born to our class, our privilege, our norms, and our expectations.

Like it could have *never* been otherwise.

But maybe we get the first wisp of gospel in this small detail: Someone has noticed one of the least of these . . . Boaz, a man of wealth and worth, had noticed a Moabite woman with not much more to her name than her destitute mother-in-law. And maybe, somehow or other, Boaz could see, could imagine the world as it might have been, if things had been otherwise.

According to the text, Boaz doesn't pray. Doesn't join the choir. Doesn't go to seminary. What does Boaz do? The text reports that Boaz calls a meeting out at the city gate, the place where ancients would conduct public business. Not religious business, but the business of business. And lo and behold, as it happens, Boaz sees So and So come strolling up the hallway of this business world. Boaz walks up, hooks his arm into So and So's arm, and pulls him along, as he whispers something like an insider's tip into his itchy ears. "Friend," he says, "I'd like to let you in on an opportunity, an opportunity of a lifetime. . . ."

So and So likes the sound of this. "Okay, I'm all ears." Boaz asks him to wait for a moment as he gets ten men together, a quorum so that he can conduct

---

[22] Schipper, *Ruth: A New Translation*, 162.

the official business of the business community. It turns out this won't be done on the sly. So and So's antennae go up, suddenly alert, maybe *exposed* to public scrutiny.

"You know Naomi," he says to So and So, "the one who went to Moab, how her husband, Elimelech, our relative died. . ."

"Oh yes, bless her heart . . . what a waste," he says.

"Indeed, such a pity" says our Boaz. "Did you know she wants to sell her property?"

"Sell her property, you say? Oh my! No surprise, really. It's just going to waste as it is now."

"Yes, and I wanted you to have the first opportunity to buy it because after all, you're next of kin. If you want to buy it, buy it. If not, I will buy it."

It didn't take long for So and So to do the math — he's been improving the property for a long time. Might as well take her public. A little cost to a lot of benefit.

"Sure," he smiles broadly, "I'll buy it! Let's make a deal!"

"Wonderful," says Boaz, but he doesn't quite meet So and So's hand, to settle the deal. There's more. He adds some small print, which is actually large print if you care about the fate of Naomi and Ruth.

"If you buy this property," he says, "in front of these witnesses, you are also taking on the responsibility of the widow Naomi, and her daughter-in-law, the Moabite, Ruth, whose husband, Mahlon, also died."

What on earth is Boaz talking about? The explanation is in the law. By law, the nearest male relative of Elimelech was obliged to marry either the widow or the widow's daughter in order to continue the family line. Remember this is a *patrilineal* system, a system that only works if there is a male descendant. Elimelech was dead. So were his sons. No one was left but these two widows, Naomi and Ruth. Naomi is beyond the age of child bearing; Ruth was the widow of Mahlon, son of Elimelech, and she is of childbearing age.

Which means . . . in So and So's estimation, any profits from this transaction would not go into his personal wealth management plan (his family line), but instead would go to the child, the son of Ruth, and thus this land and its profits, all of it goes to Elimelech's family name, not So and So's.

That's complicated so let me state it plainly: So and So wanted the privilege of property but not its social responsibility. And that's when the deal broke down. So and So walked away.

Like sometimes we are tempted to walk away . . . when broader responsibility interferes with personal privilege. Or, alternatively, like sometimes we choose to stay at the negotiating table. To speak publicly. To be as sly as a fox in dealing with powers. To call to account, to deal, to negotiate, to bargain — because mercy is not limited to church on Sunday. Mercy works in the public square as well, in its called meetings, in its city councils and in the wheeling and dealing of closed door sessions, where So and So's commit robbery under the guise of respectability.

We come to realize that the grace we enjoy through our wealth, or our status, or our education did not come cheaply and we, like Boaz, will not go cheap into the night. And maybe we also sense, somehow, someway, that our fate is tied up with the fate of the least of these. That it might have been otherwise for us. As we read this text, the narrator invites us to see the world through Naomi's eyes, as if that life might have been our life.

What does Naomi yearn for? If we take her at her own word, she yearns for security. A home. A neighborhood to call her own. She doesn't aim for a revolution. Sorry Bernie, she's just not feeling the Bern! Maybe some of us feel the revolutionary burn, but that's not what Naomi is looking for. She wants a house she can call home.

I think that's the gospel message for us — that God is revolutionary and also committed to the welfare of the city; God not only raises the dead, but teaches us ignorant pilgrims how to live better, more justly, more humanely; the gospel here is that Christ speaks not only to his disciples of heavenly things, but also of worldly things; Christ speaks not only of the power of love, but he speaks truth to those who love power.

Boaz represents a kind of public Christ for us; not the Christ of our personal piety, but the Christ of our common life.

Speaking of our common life . . . Kevin Plank, the CEO of Under Armour, plans to build a large-scale water-front community in South Baltimore, estimated to cost in the neighborhood of $5.5 billion. And Baltimore's City

Council is excited to see this go forward. Truth be told, the people of Baltimore are excited to see this go forward.

Sagamore Development, the company hired to pursue this plan, wants the city to finance part of this, to the tune of about $1.1 billion dollars. City Council is ready to schedule a $535 million-dollar tax payer funded financing scheme. It looks like a great deal, like we'll all be swimming in money. Sagamore estimates developing the area will generate a net of $40.3 million dollars annually.

Money, money, money.

But that's not fair. That So and So — I mean Sagamore — wants to include 10% of the housing as "affordable" for folks who are making less than 80% of the median income; translated that means *affordable* for a family of four that makes $65,700. Community organizers say this is not enough. Saddling the city with 40 years of debt, debt that will inevitably draw down funding for schools, for programs for at-risk kids, for public services isn't being taken into account. And even more, the deep economic inequities in Baltimore, the kinds of inequities that continue to fester today, are not being taken into account.

They want to improve a property . . . but do their plans improve our community, our humanity?

Community organizers want 20% of the housing set aside as affordable, defining *affordable* as housing that would be accessible to a family of four that makes just $26,880 annually. Sounds like a neighborhood where Naomi might actually live. Revolutionary? Maybe, maybe not. But it might be a safe and affordable place to call home.

Today's text began with the men wheeling and dealing, treating women like property, and ends with the women announcing the birth of a son . . . not to Boaz, the father, but to Naomi, a woman. Unheard of in the biblical testimony . . . except maybe for the birth of Jesus, whose birth prompts an angel to proclaim that a "child has born to us" — a child conceived by the Holy Spirit is given to us sinners. Revolutionary? I think so.

There's more. But all of it comes down to love, undomesticated, unapologetic, all-in love, a love that sacrifices self for others without glancing back.

Love is the first and truest revolutionary.

But the works of mercy, the children of love, these are produced in the field, where nameless immigrants work; on the threshing floor, under cover of darkness; and, yes, the works of mercy may also be found in the negotiating room, at city council, behind closed doors, where deals are made, where dreams are brokered . . . or sometimes betrayed not only by the So and So's of this world but those who know better.

So and So has no intention of doing anything for anyone but himself. And no one will say a word, because that's the way the world really is. The art of the deal is mostly robbery. But love, love's a revolutionary — it's Martin King thundering on high about a dream; it's a movement of people singing we will overcome; it's a congregation listening for God's word in the whirlwind of our century.

And it's Boaz, too. At the bargaining table. Boaz, if you're here today, don't rest until the matter is settled; Boaz, if you're here today, call a meeting; activate your networks; use your skill and knowledge of how power works to make a difference for the least of these; Boaz, if you're here today . . . Boaz, Naomi is praying that you won't be building a skyline of privilege or a wall of economic and ethnic segregation; she's praying that you won't look the other way; she is praying that you will think more about people than buildings, more about communities than profits.

Boaz, if you're here today. . . . don't rest until the matter is settled.

Boaz, if you're here today . . . listen . . . listen . . . somewhere in Baltimore, a Naomi dreams of having a home of her own.

Boaz, if you're here today. . . .

Amen.

July 23, 2016

Chapter Seven

A Prayer with Punch

I'm considering a preaching series on women in the biblical text, in part to address what Frances Taylor Gench calls the "textual harassment" of women in Scripture.[23] I may not be a woman, but women, especially feminist and womanist scholars, were my teachers. And I am not ashamed of the gospel as I have received it from women! Women, including my mother, have been formative for how I read Scripture. I also happen to be the father of three daughters. At the same time, I know that biblical texts have been used to silence women and I am convinced that the "assault on women" (real and symbolic) has to do, in part, with culturally approved traditions of biblical interpretation.

I want to do my part in "salvaging" the text in order to make better human beings of us all, female and male, created in God's image. I undertake this salvage operation in the spirit of one who trusts the testimony of Scripture to be good news. I find that Ellen Davis' view fits readily enough with my own: "No biblical text may be safely repudiated as a potential source of edification for the church. . . . When we think we have reached the point of zero edification, then that perception indicates that we are not reading deeply enough; we have not probed the layers of the text with sufficient care."[24] I read with something like critical trust, aware that deep readings of Scripture produce edifying results for the whole church.

Luke's parable of the widow and the unjust judge represents a text that invites reading and rereading. Luke includes a large amount of material on women, giving women more voice than any of the other gospels. This text accents a woman's determination, voice, and physical presence in a contest of power. At the same time, it is about the church, too. The story of the widow who seeks justice from the judge who judges (consistently and characteristically) unjustly speaks in a different key about the prayers of the church and perhaps of the

---

[23] Frances Taylor Gench, *Encountering God in Tyrannical Texts: Reflections on Paul, Women, and the Authority of Scripture* (Louisville: Westminster John Knox Press, 2015), 2.
[24] Ellen F. Davis, "Critical Traditioning: Seeking an Inner Biblical Hermeneutic" in *The Art of Reading Scripture*, ed. Ellen F. Davis and Richard B. Hays (Grand Rapids: Wm. B. Eerdmans Publishing Co., 2003), 164 quoted in Frances Taylor Gench, *Encountering God in Tyrannical Texts: Reflections on Paul, Women, and the Authority of Scripture* (Louisville: Westminster John Knox Press, 2015), 2.

persistence of the powerless, as they pursue God's justice: "Justice, and only justice, you shall pursue" (Deuteronomy 16:20).

According to Elizabeth V. Dowling, Scripture portrays widows as uniquely powerless and vulnerable to exploitation (Exodus 22:22-24; Deut. 10:18; 24:17; Psalm 68:5). And yet, according to Dowling, the widow is anything but helpless. One person notes the widow's resolute and dogged exhibition of what might be called "bitchiness."[25] For her part, Dowling rejects that characterization as undermining of what the widow actually achieves, namely justice: "She takes the initiative and cries out for justice until she achieves it. She acts on her own behalf, asserting herself, and by her words eventually prevails. The woman uses what she has, her voice and her time, to challenge the injustice."[26] Certainly, she achieves justice. But isn't it also possible that the judge who judges unjustly might have spoken of her in precisely these terms? And perhaps those who oppose justice speak of the church that is relentless in its pursuit of justice in this way as well.

My own sense of this parable is that the woman supplies a figure for the church, a model for its testimony and its practice. It also helps us to see the courage of those who represent the pleas for justice and equity in our public square. At the same time, it pushes us to recover a posture of prayer that might not be welcomed as prayer in the "courtroom of public opinion" but it is prayer, even if it is prayer with a punch.

Sermon

> *Then Jesus told them a parable about their need to pray always and not to lose heart. He said, "In a certain city there was a judge who neither feared God nor had respect for people. In that city there was a widow who kept coming to him and saying, 'Grant me justice against my opponent.' For a while he refused; but later he said to himself, 'Though I have no fear of God and no respect for anyone, yet because this widow keeps bothering me, I will grant her justice, so that she may not wear me out by continually coming.'" And the Lord said, "Listen to what the unjust judge says. And will not God grant justice to his chosen ones who cry to him day and night? Will he delay long in helping them? I tell you, he will quickly grant justice to them. And yet, when the Son of Man comes, will he find faith on earth?"*

> — Luke 18:1-8

---

[25] Robert M. Price, *The Widow Traditions in Luke-Acts: A Feminist Critical Scrutiny*, SBLDS 155 (Atlanta: Scholars Press, 1997), 198.
[26] Elizabeth V. Dowling, *Taking Away the Pound: Women, Theology and the Parable of the Pounds in the Gospel of Luke* (New York: T&T Clark International, 2007), 183-4.

Luke gives us the context for today's text, a face-off between the widow and an unjust judge. The point of the text is a lesson in God's faithfulness, which, given the parable — the unjust judge being analogous to God — might be difficult to keep in sight. Additionally, we don't think of prayer through the lens of a courtroom, as a space of contesting claims, but that's what we've got in front of us today, so let's dive in.

The widow's petitions — her prayers — face an uphill battle. It's an uneven match. Her odds don't look good. She doesn't have a lawyer. In her culture, her odds would be better if she had a son or a new husband to represent her in court. She doesn't. She is a widow. Helpless. And she is representing herself. We don't know precisely the nature of her complaint. We do know that it was not uncommon for women, particularly widows, to be deprived of their legal rights. Without a husband or a son to represent her rights, the rights of widows were often ignored, without fear of prosecution. So our widow seeks her day in court — not to punish the accused but rather to plead with a judge to vindicate her rights. Maybe this is something like a "small claims" court. It has to do, probably, with properties or resources to which she was entitled but which were being denied to her. In the world's estimation, it was probably a pittance, but to her maybe it made the difference between security and grinding poverty.

Perhaps if the system worked the way it was supposed to work, and the judge ruled with equity and justice and reflected Israel's ideal of someone who regarded the rights of the widow, the orphan, the alien, everything would have worked out okay. But he isn't that kind of judge. He is a far cry from the ideal judge, the judge who judges with equity — this judge judges unjustly, to translate the text literally. This judge does not fear God, which is like saying the judge doesn't care that God may judge him. And he doesn't care for human beings, much less a widow, who might have more in common with an insect than an actual person with whom he might have to deal. It's an uneven match. He represents not just an individual but a system. And it seems that the system is utterly implacable, far above anything like criticism or accountability; certainly, it is not accountable to the lowly complaints of a widow, a no one and a nobody.

We know something about unjust powers. Unscrupulous actors — people who don't care about God or neighbor. People who can boast about sexual assault, then toss it off as "locker room" talk, invoking a kind of immunity that would never pass muster anywhere else except on national television. Earlier that same day, The Candidate gathered together women to accuse the female candidate of her *husband's* crimes against women.

Was that supposed to impugn her or "normalize" sexual violence against women? Or both? Folks, we're talking about sexual assault, an act of violence, and it's being turned into a circus. Or it was turned into a circus a long time ago; we're just getting to view the newest installment . . . and apparently, the ratings are through the roof. Meanwhile, pre-adolescent girls and boys watch the live stream of this whole thing, much of which would be more appropriate in a closed-circuit courtroom, but now it's on front page news for everyone.

We think this is about a vote between a Democrat and a Republican. So be it. Yet who, we might ask, represents our children or our neighbor's children in this debate? Who represents the boys and girls who view this back and forth? Who represents the young teens watching this, who are trying to figure this thing out? "Do I have a right speak out?" they wonder. "What was that experience? Was that my fault?" Why are women shamed for sexual assault? Aren't they the victims? It's got to be confusing.

Some of you know that I expressed reservations about having our children, our daughters specifically, watch the presidential debate last Sunday. Ultimately, our girls watched, and I am hopeful that they won't lose faith in our democratic process. We'd started reading the U.S. Constitution together and now I'm determined to continue doing that with them. It's a beautiful document. It's as much aspirational as it is foundational to our form of government.

But our democracy, as it is now, is profoundly flawed. And this recent business, as shameful as it is, is just one piece of a much larger and profoundly sick system. And yet, our ability to change that system seems implausible. And it's a bigger problem than the voting booth, though that's important. It's bigger in part, because we know that such things can be said with impunity because the world has been willing to look the other way for a very long time. The unjust judge had been judging unjustly long before he ever met the widow. And this is the hard truth: after November 8th — whatever happens — this is the world we will continue to live in. And in the meantime, I think we should ask ourselves who represented a young girl watching last Sunday's presidential debate? Who represents a little boy who views this thing? That a figure who would send our children into harm's way, this person can say what he says without a trace of shame or actual contrition?

No one represented the widow in this text. And we know what happens to most widows. Maybe they begin with determination. But eventually, they wear down, they give up, their resources exhausted. They can't continue the fight. That's the way it mostly happens. But today's text shows an unlikely outcome. The unjust judge doesn't cease to be unjust. Instead, he recognizes that this woman might actually give him a black eye. That's the literal translation of the text. Instead of "wearing him down" (as in most translations) Luke's Jesus uses a boxing term, a term from the boxing ring, to name the worry of the unjust judge.[27]

Luke's Jesus ends up mixing metaphors, throwing us off balance. The unjust judge worries in his own mind that she will deliver a blow just beneath the eye. He worries that she's going to land a strong right hook or deliver a left jab — and that is what makes him rule in her favor. He doesn't care about justice. He doesn't care about her. He cares about himself. His own comfort. Remember, we're talking about prayer here and therefore about God and the basic theological claim is that if bad actors can do the right thing for the wrong reasons, we know even more that the good God will do the right things for the right reasons. Amen? That reflects our faith in God.

But I can't escape the metaphor of the boxing ring/courtroom that Luke employs in today's text. Jesus uses this to teach us something about prayer. We pray for our leaders. Maybe our prayers should have a bit more punch in them than they do.

Now this requires some unpacking, especially given Jesus' insistence that we love our enemies. Don't remember anywhere where he encourages us to give our opponent, just or unjust, a black eye. Interestingly, this is not what actually happens in the text. The unjust judge is, in a sense, psyched out. This, I discovered, is part of the artistry of the boxing ring. It's not merely about fighting, though it is that; it is also about fighters who adopt what one person calls the "physiognomy of astuteness" — the physical stance of alertness, of focus, of determination.

It's not unlike the body of a person in prayer — ready, as it were, for contact, for holy encounter. The novelist Joyce Carol Oates, who says she is no admirer of boxing, nevertheless describes the boxing ring in ways that suggest the very antithesis of the courtroom: "The boxing ring is an altar of sorts," she writes, "one of those legendary spaces where the laws of a nation are [momentarily] suspended. . . ."[28]

---

[27] R. Alan Culpepper, "The Gospel of Luke" in *The New Interpreter's Bible*, vol. 9 (Nashville: Abingdon Press, 1995), 338.
[28] Joyce Carol Oates, *On Boxing* (Garden City: Dolphin/Doubleday, 1986) quoted in Anatole Broyard, "A Review" in *The New York Times* (15 March 1987), accessed on June 4, 2018 at https://archive.nytimes.com/www.nytimes.com/books/98/07/05/specials/oates-boxing.html?_r=1.

Entering the struggle for the good is like that because you enter a place where neither the good nor the evil exercises perfect dominion. It's liminal space. Entering the ring releases something like "animal dread" — dread of a devastating blow. When the widow enters the ring, she forms her testimony out of the song of Scripture. She sighs and pants and sings for God's justice; in her hands, she holds reams of evidence and in her heart, she holds the conviction of God's justice. When she enters the ring, she enters with a sense of poise.

Think of Muhammad Ali. I don't remember any of his punches, though I'm sure they were real enough. What I remember was his dancing in the ring, almost showing off his legs, lunging and then suddenly dancing back from his opponent. That was his strength — his body as poetry. There was a punch too but, without that poetry, would Ali be the boxer he was or the moral inspiration and courage he represents even to this day?

Here's the message of Luke: Show up at the rally. And at the voting booth. Pray to God and testify for the sake of the least of these. Enter, physically, into a space of contest. I think of those who have shown up to political rallies — a Muslim woman in traditional garb at one of Trump's extremist rallies, or a group of people who showed up to protect the friends and family of the victims at the Pulse Club in Orlando. They showed up dressed as angels and created a wall of compassion to surround the people who were grieving the deaths of their loved ones. These "angels" weren't the ones grieving, but they were testifying against hate; that counter-testifying community showed up to contest the hate-slinging slogans of extremist Christians — a counter-testifying community who knew justice and loved justice and showed mercy and prayed with their bodies — showed up almost like the widow shows up and speaks up, in the face of the unjust judge, against seemingly implacable and mob-like aggression. These odd ones out show up and they stand out, and they get shouted down, sometimes they get assaulted, they are the objects of verbal abuse. They pray with their bodies and their bodies are sometimes battered. *Battered because of what they pray, where they pray, why they pray, for whom they pray.*

They do not so much "strike" out as awaken the fear of the unjust judge that he will be exposed for what he is — this, too, is the spirit of Christian prayer. It tells the truth. In her book, *A Woman Reads the Gospel of Luke*, Loretta Dornisch says that Luke creates an interesting "construct" for thinking about prayer. It is not simply asking for things. Or seeking some kind of therapeutic relief. Prayer may hold these meanings for us. Yet, prayer is not confined to the pious sigh. Prayer consists of "commitment and vow and dedication."[29] The widow's insistence that the unjust judge do justice emerges from the Lord's Prayer, which is both the prayer of the pious but also the prayer of the afflicted:

> *Thy kingdom come, thy will be done,*
> *on earth as it is in heaven.*

We do not pray, *may* your kingdom come, and *perhaps* your will be done — if the stars line-up. Faith driven prayer arises from something like thirst, something like the way we thirst while water is near to our lips. We can almost taste the kingdom. Her pleas to the unjust judge grow from her unshakeable faith in God's steadfast love.

Prayer, in this account, reflects a worldly struggle that proceeds from the strength of our convictions. Maybe you've heard the story of an elderly African American pastor who stood up and offered a one sentence interpretation of today's parable: "Until you have stood for years knocking at a locked door, your knuckles bleeding, you do not know what prayer is."

At the end of today's text, Jesus asks, "Will I find faith on earth when I return?" Or will Christ find our knuckles bloody with persistence?

Jesus asks us whether or not he will find a church that prays with the piety of the widow — prays night and day, prays without ceasing — as well as a church that demands God's justice from unjust powers, insisting on justice in the strength of its faith in God's justice, in God's peace. A church whose prayer grows out of dedication, vow, and commitment.

Maybe we've got a left jab dancing in the margins of our prayer book . . . maybe it's about time we got in the ring. Our little girls and our little boys . . . they're watching this drama, they're listening, they're saying their bed-time prayers.

And so must we. Amen.

October 16, 2016

---

[29] Loretta Dornisch, *A Woman Reads the Gospel of Luke* (Collegeville: The Liturgical Press, 1996), 186.

Chapter Eight

An Opportunity to Testify

Many who lived through 9-11, or the Challenger Disaster, or another catastrophic event can recall exactly where they were when the news broke. The day after Trump's election, I was driving to the church, down Mt. Royal Avenue. As I listened to the news, I replayed the things that had been said by then "Candidate Trump" — I replayed them and a feeling of slow dread came over me. I was still numb, really. You pass through such days or such days pass through you, leaving the skid marks of what feels like a disaster happening in slow motion. And Sunday was coming — fast!

As I prepared for Sunday, the lectionary delivered up Luke 21:5-19. It was one of those Sundays when you realize that the news has overtaken the attention of the congregation. That happened more often in 2016-2017 than I had expected. Mostly, even on those occasions when the nation was coping with some crisis, I preached whatever text was given to me in the lectionary. Once or twice, I left the lectionary. Mostly, not. Mostly, the lectionary was not so much "fitting" as it was rich, polyvalent, capable of shouldering the day's events. This sermon represents an attempt at salvage — healing, sorting, finding the ground beneath our feet. A lot of my preaching over the past two years has been in that key.

Luke's Jesus says that in the wake of catastrophic loss, you will have an "opportunity to testify" — it struck me then and it strikes me now as a difficult, if not impossible command to fulfill. What kind of opportunity does the election of a demagogue give us? As I thought about my own reactions, I recalled the way the church had gathered in our small chapel, to pray. Communities around the country surely did the same thing. But I also joined a march that started at the Washington Monument and ended at the Inner Harbor — again, with police helicopters above, search lights flashing in our eyes. As the crowds dissolved into another night, and I made my way home, I noticed a stranger stopping to help another stranger. A conversation ensued between them. I guess I thought that this must be what it means to testify, to be grounded enough in the present, with the real needs of real people, that you could respond. That's what distinguishes a people tossed by every wind and rumor and a people who are grounded on a rock of confessing God's faithfulness. We may be caught up in the upheaval of our age, but God is not far from us . . . nor we from God.

One more thing . . . this sermon was preached on the occasion of a baptism by confession of faith. In the upheaval of our nation, our church gathered around the font to welcome the newest member of Christ's church. It was an almost passing event, something I even struggle to remember given the events of that week. But it was perhaps more important than the election, than the fear — by God's grace, on that Sunday of national unease, God stirred the waters of our identity with testimony to our past, present, and future hope in Christ.

Sermon

> *When some were speaking about the temple, how it was adorned with beautiful stones and gifts to God, Jesus said, "As for these things that you see, the days will come when not one stone will be left upon another; all will be thrown down." They asked him, "Teacher, when will this be, and what will be the sign that this is about to take place?" And he said, "Beware that you are not led astray; for many will come in my name, and say, 'I am he!' and 'The time is near!' Do not go after them. When you hear of wars and insurrections, do not be terrified; for these things must take place first, but the end will not follow immediately." Then he said to them, "Nation will rise against nation, and kingdom against kingdom; there will be great earthquakes, and in various places, famines and plagues; and there will be dreadful portents and great signs from heaven. But before this occurs, they will arrest you and persecute you; they will hand you over to the synagogue and prisons, and you will be brought before kings and governors because of my name. This will give you an opportunity to testify. So make up your minds not to prepare your defense in advance; for I will give you words and a wisdom that none of your opponents will be able to withstand or contradict. You will be betrayed even by parents and brothers, by relatives and friends; and they will put some of you to death. You will be hated by all because of my name. But not a hair of your head will perish. By your endurance you will gain your souls."*

— Luke 21:5-19

How are you feeling, church? A Civil Rights activist used to ask her groups after an act of civil disobedience, "Where does it hurt?" Another version of the same question: "How is it with your soul?" Is your passport up to date? I hear Canada is bracing itself for a mass exodus out of the United States. Any of you thinking of booking a ticket out? Could you perhaps squeeze me into one of your bags? After Tuesday's election, we're feeling a bit confused. On Wednesday, we woke up to, brace yourself . . . *Trump's America*.

How does that make you feel . . . confused? Betrayed? Angry? Scared? Depressed? Ashamed? Nauseous? Raw? Happy?

[Here a long-time member of church and an enthusiastic Trump supporter, cried out jubilantly, "Happy!"]

I know this is First & Franklin, but there is one, and probably more, who are thrilled or at least satisfied with Tuesday's election. You may imagine that this is much ado about nothing. You win some and you lose some. And the truth is that our Democratic leaders, including President Obama, have encouraged us as a people to gather around the President-Elect. Give him a chance. Honestly, I want to, but I'm not so sure. A lot of this depends on the idea that he will not make good on all his rhetoric — that words don't matter. I'm a theologian of the book. Words matter for me. Every jot, tittle, and twit. But I'm told he doesn't really mean any of it . . . the ban on Muslims, the mockery of people with disabilities, the boasts of sexual assault . . . it was just talk; or maybe he's just keeping us in suspense?

Be that as it may . . . being disappointed in the outcome of an election is the norm rather than the exception. Even when your candidate wins, feeling a level of disappointment is normal. I can live with disappointment. I disappoint myself every day — what's one more disappointment? *But this feels different.* This feels like dismay for over half the country that did not vote for the President-Elect. This feels like stunned disbelief, as in this can't be happening, but, my God — and I use that expression intentionally — it is happening before our very eyes. This feels different. And it looks different too, on the ground. On Thursday, some of us gathered for prayer in Reid Chapel. About fifteen or so people from this community came together. People were and probably still are hurting.

One person told me she felt as if someone had hit her in the stomach. Put another away, she came into Reid Chapel describing herself as the victim of an assault — many women have used this language, particularly of this President-Elect. So maybe that is how some came to pray in Reid Chapel. As if victims of assault. At the same time, as we gathered to pray, a protest was taking shape just down the street, at the Washington Monument. While there were prayers in Reid, there were angry shouts on Charles Street; while there were songs of faith in the chapel, there were slogans and chants on the street.

This feels different because, perhaps, it is different.

Luke's Jesus doesn't know anything about Trump, but he does know a thing or two about dismay or how it impacts us. The temple, according to Jesus, will be destroyed. Since it's not our temple, we may not feel it, but for those who heard Jesus, that message must have hit them hard. The temple reflected God's glory here on earth. It was the physical representation of God's divine plan. It could not be moved. Its foundations ran deep into the memory of Israel. Its ceilings lifted the eyes of worshippers heavenward, as if they were ancient telescopes bringing heaven a little nearer to earth and earth a little nearer to heaven. And it was beautiful. And it would be destroyed. Indeed, it was destroyed in 70 C.E. by the Roman Empire. And this is probably what Luke has in mind, the Roman destruction of the temple. But the text itself is looking ahead to what hasn't happened yet but will happen. The people who heard Jesus say these things wanted to know when it would happen and what to look for. Jesus' answer might not give us a lot of comfort, at least not initially. He warns us: Beware. Be on the look-out. Keep your eyes open and your minds alert.

Many will come saying "I am the One" — the savior, the one who can do what no one else can do — many will say that now is the time, this is the hour when we will finally and decisively achieve a victory, a change, a final solution.

Don't go along with the crowd. Don't follow them. Don't join their Twitter feed. Don't wait in suspense for their decisions. Don't. Just don't.

But it's not going to be easy. These kinds of powers cast their spell in times of deep social unrest. Jesus paints a picture of a world in turmoil. Not just earthquakes, but great earthquakes; not just unease, but terror. Not just the brightening of a distant star, but terrible portents and awful signs from heaven. Not just a shortage here or there, but famine and plague, a contagion that blows through firewalls of security and sanity as if they were nothing. As if that were not enough, to the creational disturbance, Jesus adds the political. Kingdom will rise up against kingdom. There will be persecution. People will hate you because of my name. You will be thrown in prison. Some of you will be killed. With the stars shaken from their places, with the convulsions and disturbance within this text, you might have missed the good news: Jesus says this will give you an opportunity to testify.

Let me just say, as a preacher, I would rather not preach amid the crisis we have seen in the past week. Ordinarily, I like the library for thinking through texts, but this week was different. This week, it wasn't the library but the streets that framed my thinking. After our Service of Prayer in Reid Chapel, I struck off down the street, on foot, down to the Washington Monument. And there was the protest that was starting. I joined. Maybe I felt like a tree, pulled for a moment from its tether to the establishment, from this pulpit eight feet above contradiction, pulled along by this rush of movement. We took over Charles Street (I've always wanted to "take over" a street!).

I am your pastor, but at that moment, I was also a protester. Walking between cars. Sometimes chanting. I didn't have a sign, but I probably stood out, as a middle-aged guy in what looked to me like a sea of youth, their shouts and chants echoing in random ways, without a center, except for the force of movement itself, except for the anger, the dismay that haunted us that night. . . . And then, about thirty or so minutes later, it was over.

Or it was over for me. I began walking back, by myself, before the protest had ended. I walked up Charles Street. It was interesting to me that joining the march allowed me, for a moment, to feel like I was reversing what was happening. I felt the thrill of movement, of organizing. I didn't give myself entirely to the march; I would say I drifted with it. I'm glad I joined it. But something happened as I walked back, still engrossed in that experience. A woman, a homeless friend, was struggling with all her worldly belongings — I only noticed her vaguely, which is to say, barely at all. But in my half-awareness, I saw a man stop (odd, I thought) to ask her a question: "How far are you going?" he asked her, as he pointed at her bags.

I didn't hear the answer. But when I turned back, I saw him carrying her bags, as they slowly walked, visiting together, down Charles Street. I thought about that — did we see her when we came down Charles Street? Could we have seen her? No. Not in a million years. We saw our upheaval. We saw our dismay. We felt the thrill of our numbers. One of the protesters played a drum as we marched. It became our heartbeat, or it competed for our hearts. By contrast, as we prayed in Reid, we also practiced the art of silence — listening, becoming aware of our feelings, our breathing, setting a space between our souls and the escalation of fear. We experienced space, distance . . . space in which we could connect with our hearts again.

Maybe it's too much to try to put all this together, but do you think it's possible that God was speaking through these very different experiences, which each have their place, but also through the mindfulness evidenced by the person who stopped to help a homeless woman?

He hadn't planned to meet her there; he hadn't said to himself, "I'm going to show kindness" — he was walking home, feeling the pull of an ordinary routine — which in some ways is much more forceful than a protest — and yet, he was present to her in a way that suggested a deeper connection to the world God so loves, a consciousness not defined by his own agenda. Jesus says that when the world we cherish comes crashing down around us, he says this will give us an opportunity to testify. He also says we will be tempted by the riptide of fear and anger and disillusionment.

It's rushing around us. You can feel it, can't you? If you don't feel it in your heart, it's everywhere on social media. Those currents are pulling at us, tugging us into anger and dismay.

But another current, Christ's divine plan, includes these troubled times. I believe that current is nothing other than Christ's love for the world; Christ's full presence in our world; Christ praying for us, in our trouble and our hope, giving us a capacity to be present amid turmoil without being taken over by it — we may feel the upheaval of our age, but even more we cling to the consolation of Christ.

Jesus assures us that by our endurance we will save our souls. I wonder if that points to the preservation of the quality of human character — that we choose, again and again, the deeper current of compassion, justice, human dignity, care, patience, kindness; even when all around us the rivers of intolerance, callous routine, cruel efficiency, anger, shame, and blame; even when these raging currents flood the airwaves of human consciousness, we still nurture the quality of discipleship.

How do we cultivate that quality of human character, that chooses, almost without thinking, the wisdom of Christ? Luke's Jesus says, "don't prepare ahead of time what you will say — trust in God."

Maybe choosing the wisdom of Christ means trimming back on some of our social media addictions. Choose a book instead of a Twitter feed. Don't "add friends" on FB (or block them) but make friends out of strangers. Turn off the I-pod. Practice quietness. Stand still without moving. Feel awe. Do less but do what you do with great care. Quantity, writes Dietrich Bonhoeffer, competes for space. Quality, by contrast, deepens space.[30]

Our first reading was from Isaiah — remember its vision? The wolf and the lamb will feed together; the lion shall eat straw like the ox. We're far from realizing that vision. But when one of us stops being what we are told to be — consumers, professionals, commuters, Democrats or Republicans — to be the people God calls us to be, we may have to stop behaving the way lions are accustomed to behaving; we may have to stop reacting the way sheep respond when they find themselves in fearful circumstances; we may have to

---

[30] Dietrich Bonhoeffer, *Letters and Papers from Prison* in *Dietrich Bonhoeffer Works*, vol. 8 (Minneapolis: Fortress Press, 2010), 48.

change our eating habits, instead of devouring the poor in the name of a good deal, spend time working for a living wage as we do shopping for the best price.

One way we can begin to that is by helping one of our homeless friends with a brown bag.[31] It's a little thing. But little things matter, especially when they are done in faith. Carrying one of these bags to share on the street softens us, exposes us to the possibility that we are more than the world or even we ourselves imagined.

I'm glad I joined the march down Charles Street. But I'm also glad that I prayed, sang, laughed, and wept with the saints on Madison Street. I'm glad that I added my body to the unrest of this city and nation, feeling for a while its heartache. I'm also glad that here in this place, we still pray for mercy. We still pray for peace . . . we still pray for those we may call enemies. A deeper current holds us fast, here and, yes, on our commutes, in our homes, and on our streets. This morning, our choir's procession was led by two members of this church. They were marching, if you like, down the center of First & Franklin Street.

And as they marched, they held two pitchers of water. They added these waters to our baptismal font as we sang our gathering hymn, a little river of praise, its current guiding us through our worship today. We are like the people of Israel; we have been pulled out of the waters of turmoil. We have passed through rivers of fear. We have answered the God who calls us by name. We have known the riptides of trouble; we have felt the seductive power of discouragement. We have even gone down into the depths of the sea of turmoil. Perhaps we are there even now, waiting for rescue, crying for deliverance.

In a moment, we will witness again how God comes to us, calling us to trust in the one who stills the stormy waters; to trust in the one who did not leave his people in dismay; to trust in the one who gives us a word upon our lips and within our hearts even amid worldly dismay.

Perhaps even a word for a time such as ours. Amen.

November 13, 2016 (Sunday after election)

---

[31] One of the ministries of our church is to pack lunch bags (brown bags) with food, water, and information for people who are without shelter.

Chapter Nine

A Taste of Freedom

Prison may not be the first thing that comes to mind when you go to church on a Sunday morning — unless your church is First & Franklin. Men who have been released from prison are housed in apartments (transitional housing) on our campus, in what is now called the Henrietta Lacks House of Healing (formerly known as the Patrick Allison House). I often found Anthony (not his real name), one of its residents, working on his tan in the courtyard. He wore dark glasses, his skin tanned to a deep bronze. He ran every day. He struggled with depression, feelings of self-loathing, and anger. He saw a therapist on a regular basis. Even though he was free, he told me that he felt like a prisoner. Ironically, he reported feeling as if he were a captive more now than he did when he was in prison.

We went for coffee together. I didn't know one of us was in prison until I motioned that I needed to leave. Suddenly, he seized up, concerned, gesturing to his coffee, "Can I take this with me? There won't be a problem with that, will there?" The question startled me, but it was natural to him: after more than thirty years in prison, you get used to a world of rules, of prohibitions. The prison had leached into every pore of his existence. Prison exists both as a physical place but also a psychological force — you may leave the prison, but the prison may never actually release your mind from the power of captivity.

When Matthew's account of John's imprisonment came up in the lectionary, I thought I would get a taste of captivity from Anthony who knew prison first hand. He was happy to talk with me. Anthony knows one of the most profound expressions of human life, or the most tragic antithesis of human life, imprisonment. Think of *One Day in the Life of Ivan Denisovich*, or *Les Miserables* or the *Count of Monte Cristo*. Or think of Paul's letter to the church in Philippi, written from prison, while he was in chains; or Martin Luther King Jr.'s *Letter from the Montgomery Jail* or Henry David Thoreau's *On the Duty of Civil Disobedience*. Think more recently of Michelle Alexander's *The New Jim Crow*. Of the series, *Orange is the New Black*. Perhaps these meditations on the absence of freedom speak to us because we are, as a culture, increasingly defined by different forms of captivity.

If captivity becomes our sole experience of life, what does it mean to hear that good news is brought to the poor or that the blind see? Prison, it struck me, is a systemic form of coerced disability — enforced by the "free" upon the "captive". Another trait of captivity is the loss of control or the inability to define one's circumstances. Many of us feel the prison of consumerism, or depression, or disease. And to preach good news in such a context requires a different sense for the gospel, a capacity to hear the good news and to taste the freedom we do not yet know fully.

Perhaps there is a kind of realism to this text, in which Jesus does not speak directly to John in prison, but through messengers. Anthony was an avid reader. But if I ever suggested a book, his first question was always, "Is it true? I won't read fiction. I'll only read it if it's true." Anthony came to services a few times while he lived with us. He listened to this sermon, sitting near the back of the sanctuary, still in prison.

Sermon

> *When John heard in prison what the Messiah was doing, he sent word by his disciples and said to him, "Are you the one who is to come, or are we to wait for another?" Jesus answered them, "Go and tell John what you hear and see: the blind receive their sight, the lame walk, the lepers are cleansed, the deaf hear, the dead are raised, and the poor have good news brought to them. And blessed is anyone who takes no offense at me."*
>
> — Matthew 11:2-6

What does it mean to be in prison? What does prison mean in itself? And what is prison doing here, in the Season of Advent, with just fourteen days left until Christmas? Our lives are perhaps filled with other concerns, like, "Where should we hang the stockings?" Or, the kids, "When are we going to get a tree? When are grandad and grandma coming?" Or perhaps you're already thinking about New Year's celebrations, what you will do, when, and with whom. Such freedom to choose, to imagine, to plan our lives. And yet today's text poses a very un-Christmassy sort of question to us. What is prison? What is it like to be in prison? To what might we compare prison? Who is the captive? What is the point of the prison in today's text or in the Christian life, much less just before Christmas?

The text doesn't give a lot of information about the prison John was in. According to Matthew, John was put in prison in chapter four and he would be executed in chapter fourteen — not much more is said about it. But going to prison and being a prisoner are high definition moments in human life. It's a dramatic shift in the axis of human identity. Before, John stood as a preacher. He announced. He proclaimed. But now, that's not happening anymore. People don't wait for his messages; but he is suddenly dependent, even needy. Maybe he is confined to a cell in solitary. Or maybe the guards shackle his legs and wrists — maybe they figure he is a flight risk. Maybe. There's a lot we don't know, including the state of John's mind or even the conditions in prison; we do know that his disciples went to visit him, perhaps every day.

Perhaps, on their visits, they brought items that John the Baptist might want. Food more nourishing than what the prison gave — you know, the standard issue of watery potato soup. Perhaps with their visits they brought something to ease the bitter deprivation of prison life. They also brought news, which, to John, might have been as precious as the care packages, and maybe more so.

In that dark place, John heard news about the "works of Jesus" — these were works he had *heard* about, second-hand. This is John the Baptist, the one who baptized Jesus, the one who witnessed the Holy Spirit descend like a dove, the one who heard with his own ears God pronouncing his benediction upon Jesus, "Behold this is my son, in whom I am well pleased!" Once upon a time, perhaps he thought he would see those works with his own eyes.

Stanley Hauerwas, New Testament scholar, points out the irony of this text: John preached that Jesus would bring freedom to the captives — and yet, now, John is in prison. Evidently, something didn't go according to plan.[32]

So, as he takes a care package from one of his disciples, he slips him a message to give to directly to Jesus: "Are you the one to come or should we wait for another?" Apparently, John has got time on his hands. He's counting the hours, the days, and perhaps even the years until freedom. And the hours, perhaps, are growing long. And the Jesus he expected isn't throwing open the prison doors anytime soon. Something has gone seriously amiss for John the Baptist or perhaps something has gone seriously awry with Jesus. Maybe he is not the one. Maybe there is another.

It's a question all of us ask, isn't it? Some days the question may be more intellectual or philosophical than others. But it becomes a more urgent question when you're facing a deep crisis — a crisis that doesn't seem to be fading away. A crisis accentuated by a prison-like experience. I've visited prison but my acquaintance with that place is limited. To find out more, I talked to one of the residents at the Patrick Allison House.[33] Anthony, not

---

[32] Stanley Hauerwas, *Matthew* in Brazos Theological Commentary on the Bible (Grand Rapids: Brazos Press, 2006), 114.
[33] Now known as the Henrietta Lacks House of Healing.

his real name, spent thirty years in prison. Among other things, he told me one of the most difficult things is not knowing what's happening on the outside, especially with family. It would be six months later that he would find out about any illness in the family. Prison places severe limits on movement, touch, what you see, what you hear. A visit, for example, may include a quick hug and a brief kiss at the beginning and end. No holding hands during the visit — that's frowned on.

Patterns in the day, he said, are also upset. Lunch is served beginning at 9:20 a.m. The cell block never sleeps. He tells me that he struggles to sleep today because it's too quiet here. As we spoke, it dawned on me that prison is many things but perhaps it wouldn't be too much to say that it is a coerced form of sensory deprivation. You're locked in a cell. When you move outside a cell, you might wear ankle bracelets. Your hands cuffed together. We've seen pictures of prisoners — captives whose heads have been covered in black masks, so that they are effectively blind.

When I asked Anthony what I take for granted as a free person, he answered flatly: "Everything!" My guess is that a person who struggles with a disability — physical or perhaps emotional — would say something similar. Prison seems to escalate and systematize the experience of disability. Everyone in prison, as prisoners, experiences himself or herself as, in a sense, disabled. But that's normal. Routine. And that disability can become deeply ingrained, as the habits of the institution persist long after the season of imprisonment itself has gone.

Jesus continued to teach and preach after John went to prison. John heard about the works of Jesus while he was in prison — maybe the works of Jesus seemed "handicap inaccessible" to John; only for the free; only for those who suffered no sensory deficiencies; only for those on the outside, but not for those on the inside. And maybe we, too, feel like that during the Christmas season. That there are no "supports" for those who are captive to disabilities of heart or mind or body or spirit. You hear it all around you. It's the happiest time of year. Yet you feel imprisoned by economic insecurity. You see the lights on the tree, but you feel the gloom in the heart. Some don't feel this — the market has rewarded them generously, and so a sermon about people with disabilities — economic, spiritual, political — may not be welcome. May not be the sermon you came to hear. Or a gospel that you're prepared to accept.

That's okay by me. I'm not called to preach so that everyone *accepts* the message of the gospel. Some days, I'm not even sure I accept the gospel. That said, I am called to preach the gospel that Christ accepts everyone. But he does it in the most audacious, pointed way possible, accepting even the least of these.

And he makes a point of it. Jesus hears the prayers of those who are in prison, those who experience disabilities. In today's text, Jesus isn't talking to a superstar athlete; Jesus does not assemble a ruling class of billionaires and generals; he does not hang around waiting for the pronouncements of so-called successful people. He sends his message to one who is in prison, incapacitated. Why? Perhaps, because, in a sense, he knows what it means to be blind, crippled, and deaf. Remember for Matthew, Jesus, the living God, has become as we are, sharing our experience of the world. Especially that experience of captivity, of limitation, of a loss of freedom. John will die in prison. Jesus will die on a cross. The scandalous thing about Jesus is not that God became human, but that God became the crucified captive.

Jesus says to John's disciples, "Go tell John what you see and what you hear . . . the blind see; the lame walk; the lepers are healed; the dead are raised; and the poor have good news proclaimed to them. And blessed is the one who does not take offense at me."

John shares something in common with the God we know in Christ. John does not enjoy the illusion of being in command or being in control — and to that extent, Jesus speaks to him a clear and true word, even God's Word. And we receive that Word only as prayer, only a snatch of song which we half remember, half understand, half guess, half believe.

God's Word does not come to us as we would expect God to come. John didn't expect God's Word to come to him in prison. But that's where it came to John. The people didn't expect God to send them a messenger like John. What's he doing in prison? What a loser! And they certainly didn't expect the likes of Jesus. He came drinking and eating with sinners and tax collectors. They were looking for the messiah but perhaps they were looking for a more stylish messiah who liked to hang out with a more fashionable, trendy set. Perhaps our Advent invitation is to train our eyes and hearts to anticipate God's coming to us in unlikely form, in unlikely clothing, in less than ideal circumstances — not when we're stylish, successful, and smart, but, for instance, on the day you got the diagnosis; the day the divorce papers were filed; the day the sentence was handed down.

Most of us imagine that somehow, some way, we can miss that dread day of sentencing; we imagine that somehow our name won't come up on the draft list, that the dire sentence of disease or ruin or confusion will be suspended indefinitely, at least for us and for those we love.

All of us nurture this illusion. Maybe it's a necessary one, to some extent. But the truth is all of us will be dead. And it's the business of getting dead that scares us most of all. It's the loss of control. The loss of freedom. Of becoming captives in our own bodies, prisoners without hope for release. [34]

Janice Jean Springer wrote about her experience of a life sentence that was handed down to her: Parkinson's Disease. "There have been many losses," she writes but among these losses, she counts the erosion of her "self-image as a strong and vibrant woman" as the most painful. By contrast, the struggle to keep her balance, to not fall, seems all too familiar. She has lost other things as well: "I've lost my illusions. I've lost the illusion that I am exempt from the losses and limits that besiege other people." She writes that each of us will be confronted by losses that make us wrestle with the question: "[How] can I be faithful in my new circumstances?"

Springer's spiritual director suggested that her experiences might actually be giving her life a "contemplative shape, a deeper monastic spirit." What did she do? Looking at her daily schedule with a new set of eyes, she saw something that might resemble the monastic practice of praying the hours: "I inserted the Latin names of the hours of prayer into my daily routine of pills and naps and exercises. Now, each time I check the schedule I'm reminded that my day is permeated with prayer." She admits that some days it doesn't work. Sometimes she would rather enjoy a Ben and Jerry's New York Super Fudge Chunk ice cream than "[learn] what this illness" has to teach her. But on most days, on the unfamiliar road, she is given glimpses of the God she knows, her hours filled with quiet recognitions of a God of love and grace, a companion who walks the road with her.[35]

Maybe what it means to know Christ's freedom is to in a sense "taste" his presence through an awakened and spiritually enlivened imagination.

"O taste and see that the Lord is good!" Tell your soul, the captive one, the fretful one, the ashamed one, the crippled one, the nameless one, the depressed one, the despairing one, the one who is downcast and broken-hearted within you — cry out to that one, O my soul, my beloved, my

---

[34] This and the following material is adapted from Robert Hoch, "Commentary on Luke 21:25-36" (29 November 2015) in *WorkingPreacher.org* accessed on June 4, 2018 at http://www.workingpreacher.org/preaching.aspx?commentary_id=2692.

[35] Janice Jean Springer, "Illness as Hermitage" in *Christian Century* (16 September 2015), 10-1.

companion, why are you so disturbed within me? Why are you downcast? Hope in God for I will yet praise him, my savior and my God!

The world turned on its axis on the day of sentencing, on the day of eviction, on the day diagnosis. But friends, Jesus says, I have come. I am coming. And I will come again. And the world is about to turn — from captivity to freedom; from despair to hope; from darkness to the light of day, from tears to rejoicing. Amen.

December 11, 2016

Chapter Ten

For the Time Being

Among Christian progressives, it's not unusual to find something like embarrassment about Jesus. Jesus as moral example or Jesus as fried egg — either one would be more palatable than Jesus as Savior, Son of God, Messiah. We are almost phobic when it comes to grandiose claims about anything or anyone, including (and perhaps especially) Jesus. As modern rationalists, we're just not ready to take the confessional plunge! The allusion to baptism is intentional: in the accounts of Jesus' baptism we get the full awkwardness of the Christian confession, "Christ, who knew no sin, became sin for our sake" (2 Corinthians 5:21). There is so much in that statement that doesn't make sense to us . . . or even to John, the one who baptized.[36] He might have baptized Jesus without complaint had Jesus been a moral example only. Or a fried egg. But because he saw Jesus as the Messiah, he knew that he was in over his head.

John's doubt arose not from the sophisticate's skepticism but from the prophet's moral (and theological) clarity. We know this because Matthew gives voice to John's ambivalence to underscore the way in which the messianic promise would be fulfilled in Jesus Christ, the one beloved of God our Mother and Father.

Maybe we think John surrendered his ambivalence. That might be the case, but then how would we explain his questions while he was in prison (Matthew 11:2-6)? Perhaps as he sent his disciples to question Jesus further, he was asking for some kind of abstract confirmation: are you the one or is another coming? Maybe John's question speaks to the progressive's reticence — the jury is still out! The comparison isn't exact. John has already taken the plunge, leading to prison and even unto death. He asks the question from the belly of the whale, so to speak. In any case, Jesus didn't answer his question by confirming his identity but by reminding him of his deeds: the blind see, the lame walk, the poor have good news brought to them.

We don't know how John responded to those reports while he was in prison, but in Matthew's account of his baptism of Jesus, we get a hint: John consents. The "consent" doesn't get a blow-by-blow description in Matthew, only its aftermath: ". . . suddenly the heavens were opened to him" (16b).

---

[36] Notice that Jesus' baptism is omitted in the Apostle's Creed.

One wonders if, while in prison, John closed his eyes and saw the heavens open, heard God speaking, felt the Spirit confirming his calling.

Wouldn't we all like that sort of confirmation? Those visions may or may not be given to us. Baptism signifies vocation and my prior calling as a seminary professor played a part in this sermon: How did I come to take up a pastor's calling, after nearly two decades in theological education? I would like to say that the heavens opened up to me, the Spirit alighted upon me, and I knew the way I should go. I didn't. And I don't. And in all likelihood, I won't. But I think I was willing to consent to the possibility, the feeling that God was calling me to stand in these waters, with this people, at this hour.

Don Knapp, who appears in this sermon, was a tall, lanky octogenarian. For a time, he helped in the children's education program. By training, he was an engineer and I guess he would have probably been more comfortable in an adult study than with a group of small children. But when I asked him if he would be willing to serve in this way, he simply said, "Sure." Around that time, Don was diagnosed with lung cancer. Treatments began. Still, he persevered, joining the kids in the upper room of Backus House on most Sundays. Over the following year, his health continued to decline. We saw him less and less at church. He died just about two weeks ago, as I write, on March 24, 2018. In our theology, he has completed his baptism. Until then, "we see in a mirror dimly. . . ." (1 Corinthians 13:12a).

Sermon

> *Then Jesus came from Galilee to John at the Jordan to be baptized by him. John would have prevented him, saying, "I need to be baptized by you, and do you come to me?" But Jesus answered him, "Let it be so now; for it is proper for us in this way to fulfill all righteousness." Then he consented. And when Jesus had been baptized, just as he came up from the water, suddenly the heavens were opened to him and he saw the Spirit of God descending like a dove and alighting on him. And a voice from heaven said, "This is my Son, the Beloved, with whom I am well pleased."*
>
> — Matthew 3:13-17

Jesus came from Galilee and stood at the edge of the Jordan and there was no disguising it, no dodging his intentions — he wanted to be baptized, he willed to be baptized. And not just to be baptized, but to be baptized by John in the Jordan. John resisted. John tried to prevent Jesus from coming to the water.

Maybe he was embarrassed. He goes up to Jesus and says something like, "I'm sorry, my apologies, there must be some misunderstanding — this baptism isn't for you! This is for real sinners. And this water, by the way, I've been baptizing in it all day. It's contaminated by now. You wouldn't believe the people I baptize — sex workers and drug dealers, felons and hedge fund managers — I baptize all of them and they don't mind the water mostly, because they've never been clean anyway. But you, Jesus, you're different, you're living God. Pure God. Holy God. Conceived by the Spirit God, born of the Virgin Mary God. Word made flesh God. Before the creation, God. Maybe you ought to think about a different baptism, maybe a different baptizer; perhaps a different river, a different congregation where the waters run pure; where your uniqueness can be honored; where your divinity is unimpeachable."

John tried to prevent him.

Maybe he was embarrassed by Jesus' insistence that he be baptized by John, a known sinner, in the Jordan. "To be honest, Jesus, I would just as well rather you baptized me — the greater doing unto the lesser; the teacher unto the student; the master unto the servant. That's the normal of pattern of things, don't you think?"

Odd text we have in front of us today. The early church dropped it from the Apostle's Creed: "and in Jesus Christ his only Son, our Lord, who was conceived by the Holy Spirit, born of the Virgin Mary, suffered under Pontius Pilate. . . ." The early writers of the Creed omitted the account of Jesus' baptism, an event that each of the gospel writers agree is pivotal in Jesus' ministry.[37] Along with John and with those who crafted the Creed, maybe there's something we don't like about this text. Maybe it's because we can't bracket out the implications, the ambiguities, the contradictions.

Jesus is baptized with a baptism for the repentance of sin — and yet he is without sin; John, the lesser, baptizes Jesus, the greater; the impure Jordan cleanses the pure, stainless Christ, the one conceived by the Holy Spirit. Our text today is fraught with contradictions. You can appreciate John's situation. You're in the water of your life today — and you know what it's like in that particular pond — it's messy because you're a mess. It's not water you would want anyone to drink because well it's bathwater, dirty bathwater.

---

[37] Ulrich Luz, *A Commentary: Matthew 1-7*, Wilhelm C. Linss, trans. (Minneapolis: Augsburg Fortress Press, 1989), 174-176

You wouldn't want to climb into someone else's used bathwater, would you? After our little ones had their bath, I said to the girls, ten and twelve years old, "You just use the old bathwater." No surprise, they weren't going for it. My daughters have sense, which is more than we can say for God in Jesus Christ!

It's as if God in Christ asks us to do something crazy, something that makes our skin crawl a little. "No," God says. "The water you left in your tub from last night, that's good. The water that goes drip, drip, drip through the nearly clogged passages of your heart. The waste water passing through your mind, the mental litter; the contaminated water — poisoned by too many meds and too many toxins and too many regrets — that water, that's the water I want for my baptism. And what is more, I want you to take me into those waters, those waters which, in truth, seem likely to swallow you and me whole. I want you to take me fully into those waters."

And we think we would rather not. We've got good reasons to resist, to prevent Jesus' claim on our lives. John sounds to me like Moses, who didn't quite know who was talking to him from the burning bush. When God calls Moses to deliver his people from captivity, Moses asks, "Who am I to go to Pharaoh?" Moses was a wanted man — he wasn't righteous. And everybody knew it. He knew it. And, maybe more important, he didn't know God, at least not as well as he would have liked: "Who shall I say has sent me? What is your name? Don't you have a business card or something?" That's sort of basic, isn't it?

Sounds like someone being asked to serve in the church today. You're here. You believe something about God. Not sure about the Trinity. Not sure about immaculate conception. Not sure about Jesus: teacher, sure, savior — I don't know. And then there's this business of my own life. Or the church itself — we like the community, but love's a strong word. Not sure we can go there yet! Maybe God sees us with laser-like clarity, but it's different on the human side of the burning bush. Moses was busy tending his father-in-law's flocks when he got his call — maybe he was making progress in that line work.

Maybe you are, too. You wanted to get your Ph.D. first. God says, I call you. You wanted to sort out your prayer life. God says, I send you. You were still trying to spell Presbyterian, and God says, I consecrate you. You were busy publishing your next monograph, looking for another sabbatical, raising your family in the middle of Midwestern friendly, basking in the security of tenure, and God says, Come on down to this great city called Baltimore. Maybe you've heard of it? And we say — *I say*, I'm not so sure.

All call is personal. Jesus came looking for John. Jesus comes looking for you. So, I don't mind telling you that this is personal for me. Every week, I hear sirens running up and down Madison Avenue. I write sermons, literally, with red lights of alarm and emergency flashing against the wall of my study. I was installed on the day of the Pulse shootings in Orlando, June 12, 2016. My first three months saw the acquittal of the police officers involved in the Freddie Gray death. And in November we witnessed one of the most divisive presidential elections in modern history.

Our streets turned into rivers again, rivers of unrest, not so unlike the rivers of unrest that poured through Sandtown-Winchester in April of 2015. And standing in this river, on most days, I feel more like Moses or John explaining why this isn't such a good idea — maybe, God, you should look for someone else, or look for another river, create another baptism — because the waters are troubled in here and out there.

Funny thing is when people hear my story, that I left a tenured faculty position, they almost always, say, "Why on earth would you do that? Are you crazy?" Of course, I'm crazy. But I'm also called. And so are you. Before I said yes to the call of this congregation, I phoned one my former teachers, Bob Dykstra, a professor of pastoral theology at Princeton Seminary.

We talked about the change from professor living in the Midwest to inner city, urban pastor. "Whatever transition you make," he said, "it won't seem like a clear path." He was right. It has not been a clear path, for all kinds of reasons. *I wake up with them every morning.* But I said, yes. I said, I do. I said I will with God's help.

And you did, too. On June 12th, we stood together, on the day of my installation and on the day of the Pulse shooting in Orlando, and we committed ourselves to live in this particular city, to pray here, to baptize in these streets and in this town, with this people, mixed up and not always sure what we are about. All true then, and all true now. But for the time being, we said yes. In your baptism, you said yes. When you stood before the church — and said, I do, and I will with God's help, you did just as John did.

The text says, John consented. John consented to the very first words out of Jesus' mouth in the Gospel of Matthew. "Let it be so for now, for it is proper for us in this way to fulfill all righteousness." "For us" — John cooperates or participates in the "fulfillment of all righteousness" — for us. Subjectively, for us. Only God fulfills all righteousness and yet Jesus accords to John a part in the drama of salvation for us. And John acts in obedience. He is doer of the Word. He opens his hands, takes Jesus into his arms, and they go down into the water together, buried in the troubled waters of the Jordan — some thought they might never come up again.

Matthew views this act as a glimpse into the heart of God: Christ, who had no equal, the one who is exalted in the heavens became the one buried in the bowels of the sea. Something mysterious happened with John's obedience, with his yes. Matthew doesn't give us a detailed picture of the baptism but instead gives us a vision of Christ coming up out of the water, overcoming obstacles, real and imagined.

Jesus was obedient unto death. John was obedient after the manner of Christ. John obeyed. But even then, it wasn't as if all of John's doubts were removed. Last time we saw John, he was in prison and he wasn't so sure anymore: "Are you the one who is to come or should we wait for another?"

Jesus says, "Go tell John what you see and hear: the blind receive their sight, the lame walk, the lepers are cleansed, the deaf hear, the dead are raised, and the poor have good news brought to them." Blindness, poverty, disease, disability, even death itself — and yet perhaps, like John, the blind, the poor, the dead, somehow by God's grace, they consented, and their willingness was turned to their salvation, to good news.

What's your obstacle called? Any too weak? Any too frail? Somebody too busy? Someone too poor? Some of you too rich? Any dead people here today? You don't need to raise your hand! What could prevent Jesus, the one who comes to you today, from calling your name, asking for you to respond by doing God's word? What name does this thing go by, this resistance of yours? And ours?

A member of this church, Don Knapp, many of you know him, said I could talk about him today. Thank you, Don! Don is in his eighties and he's got serious medical concerns — he informs me that when you're in your eighties, that's the only kind you get! But on Sundays, at 9:30 a.m., he's here at church with half a dozen kids in Backus House. All eighty years of him. Plenty to prevent from sitting in a circle of kids, kids bouncing off the walls, sometimes trying to climb through the windows. But most Sundays, since we started the multi-age Sunday School class, he's been there, with the kids. He consented. There's a peculiar sort of baptism taking place in Backus House. Don never told me that he *didn't want to* or that he had a sudden, inexplicable desire to teach Sunday School, but when we asked he said, I do, and I will with God's help.

For the time being.

There are others in this church who have answered in a similar way and for a similar time. Which is the only time we really have — for the time being, for such an hour as this, we may consent to something bigger than ourselves. We may yield to God's reasons rather than our own. God fulfills all righteousness; all God's deeds are completed through the obedience of the Son. All we are asked to do is to consent, for the time being.

Some days, I would prevent this call, either because of who I am or because of who you are or especially because of who God is. But by God's grace, which is tireless and insistent, I consent. Today, we consent to the power of the Spirit. We consent to the opening of the heavens and love pouring down. We consent to resurrection. We consent to the Spirit that turns this body into Christ's body. For the time being, for this hour, and in this place . . . by God's grace and with God's help, we consent . . . for the time being.

Amen.

January 8, 2017

Chapter Eleven

Pick of the Litter

I was moved by the dismay of Samuel as he watched the unraveling of King Saul. Indeed, I recognized his dismay in our congregation as it grappled with what it means to live in "Trump's America" — on most days, then and now, it feels like a disaster. Pundits and comedians, along with social media, supply a steady stream of outrage. It's a form of grief. It may be cathartic, but it is only a transient kind of catharsis. And perhaps, if it is given a free rein in our body politic, it is toxic.

It was in this respect that I was struck by the insight that God commands Samuel to continue to do his priestly duties. Grief has its own vocabulary, its own justifications, and its own needs. But grieving does not bring us to the next chapter, or it won't by itself. Obviously, God grieves; the psalmist grieves; Jesus grieves. But we also grieve as a people with hope, which means we grieve for a season, but that season ends with the resurrection dawn of Christ.

One part of our calling in life is to fulfill our responsibilities as parents, employees, spouses, church members, citizens. These duties are not romantic in any grandiose sense. They are ordinary. In essence, God says to Samuel, "Keep your day job!" But it's not merely doing our duty — if we did only that, we would never learn the lesson of Albert Speer, the civil engineer for the Third Reich, who simply did his duty. Along with many other Germans, he believed that since he did not command the evil, he was not guilty of the evil. He was simply doing his duty, building the infrastructure for evil.

Even though God commands Samuel to continue in his priestly duties, God's command goes further, much further. God commands Samuel to "anoint a king" — in effect, reclaim the radical duty within the ordinary duties of life. In God's economy, we "anoint the king" of tomorrow. As Christians, this "king" in Christ rules as an infant, from the manger; the rule we imagine for tomorrow is in fact the rule we inherit today. Among Christ's first commands is the calling of his disciples, anointing these with the vocation to form a people who were, in the eyes of the world, no people (1 Peter 2:10).

Our duty as citizens in a democracy is to, among other things, vote. Vote for the best candidate, the one we believe has articulated a vision for the welfare of the entire nation, if not the creation. Vote, we say. And yet, even more, continue to work in the spirit of the high calling of Christ, looking for Christ in the least, the last, and the lost. As in the morning prayer: "Give us such joy in living and such peace in serving Christ, that we may gratefully make use of all your blessings, and joyfully seek our risen Lord in everyone we meet." Look for Christ in the least of these. If we see Christ in nothing, we have seen Christ in all. We may even be able to pray for those who may be our enemies, as Paul, the prisoner of empire, does in his concluding charge to the saints of Philippi: "Greet every saint in Christ Jesus. The friends who are with me greet you. All the saints greet you, especially those of the emperor's household" (Philippians 4:21-22).

Sermon

> *The Lord said to Samuel, "How long will you grieve over Saul? I have rejected him from being king over Israel. Fill your horn with oil and set out; I will send you to Jesse the Bethlehemite, for I have provided for myself a king among his sons. Samuel said, "How can I go? If Saul hears of it, he will kill me."*
>
> *The Lord said to Samuel, "Do not look on his appearance or on the height of his stature . . . for the Lord does not see as mortals see; they look on outward appearance, but the Lord looks on the heart."*

—1 Samuel 16:1, 7

It may not be obvious to us, but Samuel's state of mind in chapter sixteen represents something in life that most of us will experience: that is, the failure of our best made plans. Saul was the name of Samuel's best made plan. Saul was anointed king by Samuel. Samuel, the high priest of Israel, was something like the electoral college for the kings of Israel. Saul had promise — he was the son of Kish, who is described as a man of power and wealth. Saul gained notoriety as a warrior king. He knew how to throw a spear. The people demanded a king and a king they got, but not a particularly good one. He turned out to be temperamental, given to dramatic mood swings, petulant and erratic behavior. At heart, he was a man of violence. Saul was legitimate, at least constitutionally speaking. But he was an unmitigated disaster for Israel. Samuel, who was charged with overseeing transitions of power, was despondent.

Samuel grieved over what had happened — his best made plans, his calculated risks, all of it was in disarray. That's all he could see — hindsight, they say, is twenty-twenty. We see clearly when we look back, or so we imagine. And this is the irony of the Scripture reading: the Hebrew verb "to see" appears six times in today's text. He was giving his vision to what he had lost. Our regrets may go under a different name, but the phenomenon is similar: grief sharpens the perception of regret, and perhaps, ironically, does so to the point excluding actions which could lead to a meaningful future. Regret has a way of shifting our focus to what might have been, which we see clearly, even as we perhaps struggle to see either the present or the future.

Does America look back and see the road not taken? Do we grieve for an all but lost golden age? Yes, according to Yuval Levin, a conservative scholar and political scientist. In his book, *The Fractured Republic*, he argues that Americans are mired in the past — listen to Republicans, and they pine away for the Reagan era, or pray for a revival of the morality and social order of the 1950's.[38] Listen to Democrats, he says, and they want to go back to the political idealism of the 1960's or perhaps to the Clinton years. Both parties speak the language of the Boomer generation, people born before 1950. ". . . [In America]", he says, "we've rented out our understanding of ourselves to the older baby boomers." By the year 2017, something has been lost. Some of what our political parties say is true. Some of what they say is not true. But, he says, together they miss an awful lot about what has changed in America over that time.[39] I think he's got it basically right — we're grieving over a golden age that doesn't exist anymore, if it ever existed. And maybe this regret, or our nostalgia for the past, our Make America Great Again madness, is getting in the way of a meaningful future.

Samuel seems to have felt this and he grieves — for what might have been. Samuel felt this — even when God's future came knocking on his door, even then, all he could see was the wreckage of his plans. God says to Samuel, "How long will you grieve for Saul? How long will you pour your tears into this broken vessel? How long Samuel will you grieve for what no longer exists? How long before you look at reality?" We may think this is unfair of God. And yet, Scripture tells us that God grieves. God grieved when God saw that human beings were cruel. God in Christ grieves over Israel. Jesus grieved when he learned that Lazarus, his beloved, was dead.

Grief gets its time with God. There is grief for a season, even in the life of God. But, in God's economy, only for a season and when that season is done, it's done. Jesus has a way of interrupting our grief sessions with redemption action. There's a story in the Bible. A girl has died. And the people get busy grieving. Get busy mourning. They choose their funeral hymns. But Jesus

---

[38] Yuval Levin, *The Fractured Republic* (New York: Basic Books, 2016).
[39] Robert Siegel interview with Yuval Levin, 'The Fractured Republic' Explores How Nostalgia Led To Polarized Politics" on National Public Radio (7 June 2016), accessed on June 4, 2018 at http://www.npr.org/2016/06/07/481137357/the-fractured-republic-explores-how-nostalgia-led- to-polarized-politics.

comes in as resurrection action and gets busy with living. The little girl is raised from the dead. And songs of mourning are turned into songs of rejoicing.

I see a bit of Jesus in God's message to Samuel: "How long will you grieve? Get up, get out of your funeral clothes, get out of your graveyard sorrow, and go, I'm sending you to anoint a new king." And I see a bit of us in Samuel's response: "How can I go? If madman Saul hears of it, he will kill me!" I sense a "how can I go?" mentality in the church, certainly in the country — how can I go? — Saul still holds the power, commands armies, and every twitter he posts is gobbled up like it was manna from heaven, a few crumbs to perhaps reveal where this madness will ultimately lead.

But notice how God answers Samuel. Samuel does not see the future. And God doesn't show him the future, either. God says, "Take a heifer, fill your horn with oil, and do your job. And I will show you what to do." Do your job — your day job — and I will show you in that moment what you shall do. Saul is worried that he will be killed for treason. Anointing a new king, even if the present one has gone down to his mansion in Florida, is not a good thing. So, God says, "Go under cover. Do what you typically do: go around to the villages, make your priestly visits, do your churchy thing. He won't kill you for being a priest. Don't go out as if you were going to subvert the powers — *"mud on your face, big disgrace, waving your banner all over the place"*" — [*congregation joins in singing an impromptu rendition of Queen's "We Will Rock You"*] — actually, no, that's not our text! Don't go that way; our text leads us not in the way of the flag waving revolutionary, but under cover of your day job, become an underground collaborator with the divine instigation of a new politics.

There are no miracles in today's text or in the subsequent chapters — one reader says that God has gone underground. And God calls on underground collaborators to enact an alternative politics, a new politics.[40] And maybe we just don't know what that looks like. God says I will show you. Samuel obeys God and becomes an underground collaborator for an alternative politics that, as yet, he cannot see.

Taking that path, he shows up at Jesse's house. Hillbillies, maybe. Or perhaps welfare kids in Section 8 housing. "Okay," says Samuel, looking around the boarded-up windows, the graffiti scrawl, the kids looking like frightened ghosts. "I'll try. Not sure what that means, but I'm here, I'll give it a shot."

---

[40] Francesca Aran Murphy, *1 Samuel* in The Brazos Theological Commentary on the Bible (Grand Rapids: Brazos Press, 2010), 167.

Samuel says to Jesse, "Where are your sons? Send them over." First one looks pretty good. *Eliab* — check out those calves, those pecks, and that rugged look. Steely grey eyes. Sneer of power. He's got the look of a king, our Samuel thinks, his eyes began to swell with a lust for power. And God says, "Don't look at this place, or this family, or for your future the way you usually do. Don't look at the appearance but look for the heart."

"Okay," says Samuel. Sigh. "He's not the one. Send another." So, Jesse sends another son, his second oldest Abinidab? No. Shammah? Not him either. Send another, and another, send out seven — seven sons, not one of them does God choose.

"Shoot," says Samuel. "You don't have any other sons, do you? I came out all this way, I was sure...."

"Hold your horses, Reverend, I have another. He's out watching the sheep. But I got to tell you, he doesn't really amount to much. Mostly a day dreamer. That's why I left him out there. Didn't figure you'd want that kind of boy. Plays a harp alright. Kinda' think he might join the choir. A little effeminate, if you know what I mean, but I'll get him if you want."

"I want to see him," says Samuel.

"Okay," says Jesse. "Eliab, quit your sulking, go find your baby brother — bring him over here. I don't care what you think. Don't argue with me, son, just bring him!" So, Eliab brings his baby brother. And the youngest is chosen. And somehow, he looks good, too — maybe even better than the big husky, athletic guys, who could throw the javelin. Something like music shines through David's face, and it's the song of purity and dreams and, you know, he plays a harp. And maybe as he was coming behind his brother, he was playing some music, and maybe dawdling a little bit when he spied a butterfly fluttering through the flowers, or he danced a jig to the song of the bumble bee. He didn't look much like a king. But he was chosen.

If you looked closely, you might also have seen a sling shot dangling from his waste. *This one can sing, but maybe he can fight, too*. He'll need to — he'll face giants before this story is done!

And finally, the child is named, for the first time, David. Rabbinical interpreters like to say that in the biblical story of election, Abraham was chosen by circumcision, but David was chosen by God. No one saw David coming. He didn't have the right pedigree. On his father's side, his grandmother was a sex worker. His mother's side included a migrant — you know, the folks some kings like to call rapists and drug dealers. Or illegals for short. That would be Ruth — Jesus' great grandmother, an illegal. Scholars call King David a legend from the late iron age, more myth than man.[41] But something in his story rings true for us.

Whenever my step-father went to look at a litter of puppies, he chose the one that the owner ignored. And if he didn't see what he was looking for, we went home, empty handed. We were a dog family, so I saw this more than once in my lifetime. The owner of the litter would point out the pup that had the best markings, was the biggest, the most playful — universal signs of canine promise. My step-father was always polite, but he seemed to have his eye out for something else. What was he looking for? As I studied him, it dawned on me: he always kept an eye out for the puppy that was a bit small or a little bit on its own. And that's almost always the way we arrived at the dog that would be ours — the dog whose name would become Dolly, or Benny, or Booker. That's the way he was, the way he is. But there's another side to this story. My step-father is blind in one eye — all of his life he has had a weak back. One of my lasting images of him will be of him bent double, hobbling in the house, nearly crippled by pain. The blindness and the weakness in his back isn't mysterious: he contracted polio when he was kid. The boy in the bed next to him died in an iron lung. He seldom talked about that experience — mostly, what I know came from others. But I wonder if, when we went looking for a puppy, he wasn't telling me something about life, about the gesture of providential grace in a world too taken by the determinisms of power.

These stories exist. We exist. We are such a story. The church, we are born of such a story — Paul says to us, "Not many of you were wise, not many well born, not many strong by the world standards; but God chose you so that none might boast apart from him." Maybe the grace of this text to us is twofold: on the one hand, to remind us that our weaknesses may actually be the mirror image where we see gentleness. Those who have known hurt make for strong shoulders to lean on.

On the other hand, these stories, and Christ's story, push us to go beyond the status quo. You have more than a vote to cast in this electoral cycle. In a sense, we are all in the business of "electing" a new community. But often, our electing looks no different than the world's electing — we go for the pedigree.

In fact, we build walls to fence other options out. A former student gave me

---

[41] Bruce C. Birch, "1 Samuel" in *New Interpreter's Bible* (Abingdon Press, 1998), 1099-1100.

a nativity scene. A wood sculpture of Mary and Joseph and baby Jesus. But the wise men from the east can't visit them; a wall has been built to exclude them from the congregation of Christ. That's a warning, I guess. Or alternatively, a challenge to climb the wall. Or dig under it. God continues with us, underground — or over the fence — as God continued with Samuel. Could it be that God's work of electing takes us to people and neighborhoods we don't see or imagine? This text moves us and our electing activity to consider unlikely candidates as we look at the pool of possibilities presented to us. But perhaps we should look with the eyes of the heart. With the insight of the heart, we see Christ at the rescue shelters of this world — we see Christ at women's shelters. We see Christ under the bridge. We see Christ in an underfunded public school. We see Christ . . . where perhaps, apart from God's electing, we would only see our fear of failure. Where do you see Christ? In whom do you pray that you will see Christ? Do you think we could become collaborators with an underground, jumping-the-fence sort of God? Perhaps, by God's grace, we already are. Amen.

March 26, 2017

Chapter Twelve

Growing Like Weeds

Our churches shouldn't be too manicured. They should exist as glorious weeds, cracking the concrete of oppression with the song of resurrection joy.

Or at least that is how Matthew imagines the church — and of all the gospel writers, Matthew in particular has something to say about the church. Early teachers in the church drew upon Matthew as the "first" gospel, in the sense of its thoroughly ecclesiastic bent. It is the only Gospel that refers to the people who followed Jesus as Christians. Matthew alone speaks of the church more directly than the other gospels. Historically, church leaders viewed Matthew's commission to "go and make disciples of all nations" (28:19) as the mandate of Christ to western nations to evangelize and colonize every other nationality and people. Among some Christians, that view still holds sway.

Matthew may not seem like the "liberator's" gospel — it may seem like its very opposite, in fact. But according to some scholars, we may need to re-read Matthew. Matthew isn't necessarily what the missionary age of the eighteenth, nineteenth, and early twentieth century made it. How so? If we look at the metaphors, they say, we don't find the triumphalist church, but the church of small things done with great faith.

Matthew may end on a glorious, exalted commission, but the day-to-day life of the church is glimpsed through the metaphors of small things, like yeast, salt, or a sliver of candlelight in the darkness. Or like a weed, growing where it's not supposed to grow. As my ministry has evolved, I've felt that has been confirmed, time and again. I refer in this sermon to weeds growing outside of the Federal Building here in Baltimore, the site of increasingly aggressive deportation orders by the present administration. It is the unlikely intertwining of the lives of different kinds of people, gay and straight, rich and poor, black and white. Somehow, a weed garden supports a rambunctious diversity.

The triumphal entry, which is read on Palm Sunday, includes the practice of processing into church while waving palm branches. The crowds carry these branches as they sing, "Hosanna!" Crowds are, by definition, unruly, apt to appear almost spontaneously — and they can act impulsively. We don't think of the church, with its carefully worked out choreography, as a weed. But maybe texts like this remind us of our roots in the cross.

What is the saying? "A rose by any other name would smell as sweet." Or perhaps a cross by any other name would be as bitter . . . or, by God's grace, as sweet as the aroma of salvation itself.

Sermon

> *A very large crowd spread their cloaks on the road, and others cut branches from the trees and spread them on the road. The crowds that went ahead of him and that followed were shouting, "Hosanna to the Son of David! Blessed is the one who comes in the name of the Lord! Hosanna in the highest heaven!" When Jesus entered Jerusalem, the whole city was in turmoil, asking, 'Who is this?' The crowds were saying, 'This is the prophet Jesus from Nazareth in Galilee.'*

— Matthew 21:9-11

Do you know that you can sing *Amazing Grace* to the theme song of *Gilligan's Island*? "*Amazing grace, how sweet the sound. . . .*" Fun, right? I sing it to my kids. They've never seen *Gilligan's Island*, never heard the theme song, but they still think it's funny. As in, right words, wrong song. The chirpy song doesn't go with this beautiful ode to grace. That's funny because we love irony. But maybe we also crave the song — not just the ironic wink, but the simplicity of the gospel. It's something we may yearn for.

The crowd in today's gospel have got the right words, but they're singing the wrong song. But they don't hear the irony. To begin with, they say Jesus is a prophet. They are not wrong. But they're not right either. Jesus is the prophet, which they get, but he is much more than a prophet, which they miss. In contrast to the crowd, Matthew's readers would recognize this not as a political rally, with a candidate chumming the crowd with slogans, t-shirts, and bumper sticker theology. Instead, this is a royal coronation: Matthew depicts Jesus as the king, in the line of King David, entering Jerusalem.

It's a messianic motorcade (without the bling of worldly power) announcing a victory won. That's one thing the crowd doesn't get, that Christ is king already. Another appears in the language of the crowd. They sing out "hosanna" which means, "Save us we pray!" Yet, according to one scholar, this phrase was meaningless by the time it was being chanted in the first century crowd. It was an empty slogan. It's like the way we say, "goodbye"

— it means literally, "God be with you."[42] We don't say it that way, of course. When we say, goodbye, it's more like, "Goodbye, good luck, hope you don't get hit by a truck!" A far cry from, God be with you.

That might be the burden of our text — to get us to look at the difference between the reign of God that we proclaim and our living realities. The difference between our "goodbyes" and our God be with yous; the difference between the empty hosannas of the crowd and the fulsome hosannas of the faithful.

So, to begin with, let's visit with this crowd. Matthew's gospel includes three mentions of the crowd, compared to Mark's version of the story, which includes only one reference to the crowd. Why is this significant? Matthew depends on Mark and on what's called a Q source, a document that included sayings of Jesus that existed at one time, but we only have indirect evidence of its existence now. But Matthew isn't simply a copyist; he writes as an interpreter. And so, we pay attention to details like this one: why three mentions? Perhaps the crowds were important to Matthew because, at least in today's text, the crowd includes *possible disciples*. They are also *possibly a mob*. That possibility will turn into a reality, when the same crowd that sings "hosannas" on Sunday will chant "crucify him" on Friday.[43]

But for now, at this moment, both impulses exist. As a people of faith, we don't read this text as a toss of the coin — heads you're a mob; tails you're a disciple — instead, we read the text as our confession, or proclamation. When we read Scripture, the liturgist concludes his reading saying, "This is the Word of God." And the congregation replies, "Thanks be to God." This is confession. This is not a theological coin toss.

So, we read for *formation* — as people who know what it's like to go with the crowd, but also as people who have been touched by the saving health of Jesus our Savior. And this saving health is at the heart of Jesus' peculiar politics. Today's text is a form of messianic politics. When Jesus enters Jerusalem, the city, the Roman Empire, shakes with his coming. This is the second-time Jesus has shaken the establishment. The first time he shook the establishment of Roman power was when he was still a baby in his mother's arms. Now, he shakes the city as the Lord who has turned his face towards Jerusalem, as the anointed one of God.

---

[42] M. Eugene Boring, "Matthew" in *New Interpreter's Bible*, vol. 8 (Nashville: Abingdon Press, 1995), 403.
[43] Boring, "Matthew" in *New Interpreter's Bible*, 403.

Anyone who wants to say that Jesus has no politics doesn't know Jesus — even so, his politics are peculiar. For one, he does not trade in empty slogans, though the crowd often does — they've been trained to respond to such rhetoric. Jesus doesn't shame them for singing "hosanna" — he lets them sing, even though they don't fully grasp what they are singing. Perhaps he prays for them in their singing. . . .

For another . . . Jesus' political significance is connected directly to his merciful deeds. You learn Jesus' politics by paying attention to his deeds. And what precedes today's text and what comes after are Jesus' acts of health care love. What precedes today's text and what follows are Jesus' acts of food security. What precedes today's text and what follows are nothing less than Jesus' acts of inclusive love.

When Jesus goes to the temple, in this chapter, he turns over the tables of the capitalists who had got religion and the religionists who had got capital. And who does he let into the temple, free of charge? The lame. The poor. The sick. The addicted. The outcast. The hungry. The thirsty. The homeless. The debtor. The alien. It's the house of the crucified and all his neighbors. Jesus' politics isn't a platform of ideas — even good ideas — but rather it is a narrative of faithful actions which produce together a peculiar kind of community. St. Francis said that we should preach at all times. Use words only when necessary. Jesus' politics (his community organizing) grows like a weed in the cracks of the powers and principalities.

When Jesus talked about the church, he talked about her with this less than flattering metaphor, that you will grow like a weed. You want to become a weed for Jesus? We make a lot out of being members of the church. I've been a member of the church for all of my life. I think it's done me good, mostly. I highly recommend it, mostly. But when I think of a member, I think of neatly manicured bushes on Park Avenue. But when I think of a weed, I think of some crazy exuberance for life in a place where it doesn't belong. I would rather our members were first weedy people rather than manicured people. You know, one of your pastors, back when, he used to hang out at the gay bars here in town. Other pastors and probably church folk took a dim view — hanging out with weeds — he ought to be ashamed of himself!

He did it anyway.

She's not a member of the church . . . at least not yet. But one Sunday, I was walking home down Howard, and there she was, and she took my arm and said, "I want you to meet my friends." And so, on a Sunday afternoon, she's leading me along, knocking on the doors of different businesses on that back-alley street, introducing me to her friends, handing out our bulletin, sending our love to the neighborhood.

How many of us know who works on Howard?

How many us think the dandelion is beautiful? Not sure? My children do. And maybe they're on to something. Jesus' coronation ceremony looked something like a weed looks to a Monsanto or a DuPont. They sprayed their Roman Roundup version of political poison on Jesus — they saturated the political atmosphere with alternative facts, and in 140 characters or less they promulgated their lies — but Jesus keeps rising from the dead. Almost like a weed.

Weeds show up in the darndest places. Have you ever noticed that? I think mercy shows up in the darndest places. Audacious in its exuberance. Outside the Federal Building of Baltimore. I tell you, they've got a weed problem. But they're such happy weeds. Media calls them protesters. But they pray. Hate radio calls them leftists, but they sing. Certain presidents call them professional activists, but they hug, and their babies play. And other weeds, people facing deportation orders by Immigration, Control, and Enforcement, they call these weeds who stand with them *mi hermanos y mi hermanas*. They say things like *mi casa es su casa*. And *"juntos podemos"* — *together we can!*

Singing like a tongue that doesn't belong. Like love illegal. Like love without papers.

Like love creating space where there was no space. And you? In this space? Do you have papers to be here today? Are you a Christian with a pedigree? Is it your degree? Is it your ethnicity? Is it your sexuality? Is it your income bracket? Is it your profession? Come on, show your papers. Why don't you? *Because you can't*. All of us are illegal. As illegal as God becoming sin. And there's nothing more illegal than that. And we are accessories to a resurrection experience. And this is some kind of detention center turned inside out — Jesus is raised from the dead, not as a slogan but as our savior, our health and redemption.

Mi hermanos y mi hermanas, Jesucristo dice, mi casa es su casa y juntos podemos!

Maybe you heard the story out of Amsterdam. It's a weed story. A story of coronation proclamation. But it's got a cross-shaped tragedy in the middle of it. A gay couple were set upon, attacked because they were two men holding hands. Weeds. Someone wanted to kill them. Exterminate them. And I'm sure there were DuPont and Monsanto pew-sitters and their preachers (bought and paid for) ready to support that extermination. But something like a coronation began with a Tweet, 140 characters or less. A nasty woman journalist, the very definition of a weed, called "all men (straight and gay) please to just walk hand-in-hand."

It's gone viral. Like a weed. Dutch politicians, straight and gay, women and men, children, too — holding hands.[44]

Maybe we don't always know the whole reason why or even what we sing. But maybe the dandelion's king will continue to teach us. Christ will teach us to hold hands, without apology or embarrassment — growing like weeds to the glory of God. Amen.

April 9, 2017

---

[44] "Dutch Men Walk Hand-in-Hand for Solidarity after Gay Couple Attacked" in *The Guardian* (5 April 2017) accessed on June 4, 2018 at https://www.theguardian.com/world/2017/apr/06/dutch-men-hand-in-hand-solidarity-gay-couple-attacked.

Chapter Thirteen

Do Not Cling to Me

My artist mother says that the primary image of our art is made up of the images we see every day. Georgia O'Keeffe saw flowers. Or perhaps the colors of the flowers, she wasn't sure which: "Whether the flower or the color is the focus [of the painting] I do not know. I do know that the flower is painted large to convey the experience of the flower — and what is my experience of the flower if not its color?"

In preaching, we may start with one focal point, say our experience of a young child, only to find that the ordinary image, its scale and proportions, cannot capture the experience of mystery which is conveyed beyond ordinary forms.

Perhaps John would have us meet or see Jesus in this way — we would see Jesus, but we experience something inexpressible, except as color or wonderment. John writes so that we might see Jesus but even more, that we might experience the immanence of Christ's presence in the world of things: wine, bread, vine and branch, light of the world, streams of living water, new birth. John's narrator paints Jesus "large to convey the experience" of Christ's presence. And perhaps, likewise, to help us see ourselves, beyond the norms and the fixtures which are "assigned" to us.

For me, obviously, this season of life is filled with images of people of small stature — they take up a very small place in the pew, but they claim my whole existence in ways that I would have never imagined possible. I think of them now, and I grieve that they will not always be little children. True, part of me wants them to grow up, if only because I am getting older. But another part of me, equally true, would like them to always be as they are. Yet, daily, I am compelled to let go. In this sermon, Mary spoke to me, her experience of Jesus, letting go, and being formed in the inexpressible color of resurrection. But I also thought of the kind of change being wrought in her by Christ — she becomes John's first preacher not by holding on but by letting go. What did she let go of in terms of her personal identity as she followed Christ into the experience of resurrection?

What sorts of things do we grieve as we change, surrendering previous self-understandings to the experience of new life? Why does the narrator use Mary's full name at the beginning (20:1) and end of this story (18)?

Sermon

> *Jesus said to her, "Do not hold on to me, because I have not yet ascended to the Father. But go to my brothers and say to them, 'I am ascending to my Father and your Father, to my God and your God.'" Mary Magdalene went and announced to the disciples, "I have seen the Lord"; and she told them that he had said these things to her.*
>
> — John 20:17-18

Iris, our four-year-old daughter, thinks I'm clingy. She doesn't use that word, but she thinks it all the same. She refuses to hold my hand when we cross the street or walk through a parking lot. There was a time when she was happy to hold daddy's hand. Not so much anymore. Now, she screams: "You're hurting my hand" — she says this very loudly, publicly. For the record, in case child protective services are here, I am not hurting her hand; I'm holding her hand firmly.

I understand, developmentally, that she is enjoying a state of robust autonomy, which I would like to encourage. But another part of me is a tiny bit hurt. I think, somehow, I've lost something. Or maybe I am glimpsing something that I will lose one day. And maybe I do hold on a tadge more tightly than I need to.

Jesus tells Mary, "Don't cling to me." All our life, we have been schooled in the idea that we should cling to Jesus. Hold onto Jesus. Keep Jesus in your heart. But today, Jesus says to Mary Magdalene, don't cling to me, don't hold onto me. It's in the imperative voice, as in Do.Not.Cling.To.Me. That's shocking in itself; that's not the Jesus we know from Sunday School. But when we consider Mary's state of mind, Jesus' command may seem harsh as well. Mary Magdalene comes to the tomb, her mind suspended, maybe paralyzed by grief. Her teacher, her friend, her savior — he has been taken from her and she does not know where they have taken him, that is his body. She will repeat this phrase three times in today's text.

After seeing that the stone had been rolled away, she hurries back to the disciples and she uses the first-person plural: "They have taken *our* Lord out of the tomb, and *we* do not know where they have laid him" (20:2b). She will repeat it a second time, only this time in the first person singular, at verse 13: "They have taken away *my* Lord, and *I* do not know where they have laid him." And finally, she repeats a similar formula, in verse 15, to the person Jesus, who she takes to be the custodian of the cemetery, or the gardener: "Sir, if you have taken him away, tell *me* where you have laid him, and *I* will take him away." For her part, Mary, looking at the evidence, concludes that human agents have carried her Jesus away.

By contrast, the narrator hints at the God-centered action of this biblical story: the stone has been rolled away. The narrator uses the passive voice — "has been" — for the reader, this hints at a theological resolution to Mary's confusion. She saw the stone had been rolled away and concluded robbery. The passive voice hints to us, as readers, that it was not human hands, but divine power: God rolled the stone away. Similarly, the garments, folded and in their place, may be intended to remind us of the story of Lazarus, who was raised from the dead. Only in the story Lazarus, others had to remove his grave clothes for him. These grave clothes — and death itself — have been completely removed without any earthly assistance. Christ left death freely and fully and autonomously. Only God does that.

But stones and grave clothes aren't the only things being moved in this text. Mary' faith, such as it is, is being moved. Mary rises early. She goes to find a body. But the disturbed tomb upsets this journey's intended conclusion. She runs to the disciples. Her confusion disrupts their soporific resignation. They get up, they run. They look in the tomb. One of them believes and the other simply looks at the evidence. Both return to their home. They have been agitated, perhaps, but they are not yet participating in the resurrection. Their part will come, but for now, this is Mary's story. It is *her*story.

The suspense of the narrative is near to bursting by verse 15, when Jesus calls her name, "Mary" — a disturbed tomb upset her; her confusion activated the otherwise resigned disciples; now, Christ's voice spins her confusion like a top with the music of recognition. She turns and looks at this one she did not recognize and suddenly, Jesus, *her* Jesus, the one for whom she searched, stands in front of her, not a corpse, but her teacher.

And she does what anyone in her situation would do — she reached for him, to touch him. What sort of touch was this? Let me throw out one possibility: think of a group of soldiers. Perhaps in the confusion of a fire-fight, they believe they have lost of one their own. Ragged, bloodied, beaten, they try to regroup. But one of their number fails to answer. He is missing. They think the worst. It was only natural to think the worst. They grieve. They fall back from enemy lines. But then, in the night of that still raw grief, unexpectedly, the one who was MIA and presumed dead, returns, he walks into the circle of wounded and weary, seemingly a shadow but then, when his companions recognize him, something like amazement and joy overtakes them. They jump, they leap with cries of recognition, they grab him by the shoulders, slap him on the back, pull off his helmet, rub his head, hoist him up into the air, their joyful, amazed touch conveying the sense of a person returned. It's almost as if the soldiers must give this person, who had been taken from them, a body again.

Small children do this with parents. Developmentally, for a young child, absence is the equivalent of non-existence. But when the parent figure returns, the child runs to you, sometimes flings herself into your arms — your arms full of groceries, or you're barely in the door, no matter. They have got you back and they are giving you physical shape again, in some way restoring you to yourself by hugging your legs, clinging to your neck, nuzzling your cheek. Making you real again. Just in case you had forgotten who you were, and whose you are, their hugs and touch and affections, bring you back to this world.

Maybe that's what prompts this touch from Mary. It seems all good, and yet Jesus still forbids it: "Do not cling to me." Where does this come from? Why here and now? What's the significance of this prohibition? For Mary? For Jesus? For us?

Contrary to what we might think based on this text, touch and Jesus, either in his earthly life or in his resurrected state, are not mutually exclusive. Earlier in John, a woman, perhaps our Mary, washed Jesus' feet with her hair and tears, massaged scented oil into the soles of his feet. In this chapter, Jesus will say to Thomas, "Touch me and see — put your finger into my side, see the wounds of my hands." *Touch is not the problem.*

What then is the issue? We find a clue in John's theology of resurrection — with the Gospel of Mark, for example, it's enough to have an empty tomb. Christ is risen! He is risen indeed. That might do for Mark, but John adds another verb: Christ ascended. John views the resurrection as incomplete until Christ ascends to God the Father. Jesus walking around, post-crucifixion, isn't enough. John, more than any of the other gospels, underlines the abiding unity between God the Father and the Son.[45]

But that's the theological piece of this story. The other part of it must go to Mary. Why does Jesus forbid this particular touch? Mary's touch? It wasn't for Jesus' sake — if he could endure the cross, he could probably endure Mary's touch. So, then, what was it? Could it be that Mary's faith was

---

[45] Gail R. O'Day, "The Gospel of John" in *New Interpreter's Bible*, vol. 9 (Nashville: Abingdon Press, 1995), 842

authentic, but it was not complete? Maybe her belief was beginning, but it wasn't finished. Maybe Jesus' ascension foreshadows her rebirth.

The stone had been rolled away, but perhaps Mary was still in a tomb of sorts. She was stirring, but she hadn't left the tomb sealed with her tears and confusion. And that simply won't do for John. Her faith must be completed. Jesus asks her, "Whom are you looking for?" This is the same question he asks the disciples in chapter one of John. It's a critical question and it has a double meaning: you're looking for me, but also, perhaps, you are looking for your true self. For John, Mary's faith isn't completed by being a grieving woman, or by the woman who picks up the mess after all the men have gone home to sulk in their theological man-caves. And crucially, it isn't complete by picking up where she and Jesus left off, with Mary sitting at Jesus' feet, quietly taking notes. For John, her faith is perfected when she preaches, teaches, inspires, and stirs up the world God so loves.

How did this happen? Maybe she had to let go of the Jesus she remembered; but perhaps she also was beginning to see the woman she was called to become. She let go, but in letting go, she was being born anew — not of human will, or of the flesh, but of the Spirit. That's her story. *Herstory*. But what about us? What if being a student in Christ's resurrection school means that sometimes we let go in order to let God? That in letting go, something else or something within us all along, gets born anew?

George Bernard Shaw's play, entitled, Saint Joan, includes a scene in which Joan of Arc, the famous French mystic and soldier, refuses to dress in a manner that "becomes [her] sex". Her opponents question her:

> Can you suggest to us one good reason why an angel of God should give you such shameless advice [to wear men's clothing]?
>
> Why, yes: [she replied,] what can be plainer common sense? I was a soldier living among soldiers. I am a prisoner guarded by soldiers. If I were to dress as a woman, they would think of me as a woman; and then what would become of me? If I dress as a soldier they think of me as a soldier, and I can live with them as I do at home with my brothers....[46]

---

[46] George Bernard Shaw, *Saint Joan* (Baltimore: Penguin Books, 1951), 132

For Saint Joan, being thought of as a woman was, among other things, a false gender construction. She refused to "hold" onto that construction of gender. That, she said, will not give me life. She would not wear those clothes, that identity.

Iris, as I said, won't hold my hand. But I can usually coax her into holding my pinky. I'm needy that way. Of course, we all know that one day she will say that even my pinky is no longer necessary. And I'll just have to learn how to deal with that. And that's a good thing. But it occurs to me now, what other things will she need to let go of as she gets older? What will she need to let go of as a young woman, or as a woman in her fifties, or as a mother, or as a woman who is not a mother, or as a scientist, or as a woman who works in the home, or as a woman who does not, or as a woman who enjoys singleness, or as a woman who once was married, but is no longer . . . what will she need to let go of? And through all these letting goes, who will cling to her?

Perhaps if Mary teaches us today, we're letting go of a world too narrow; she teaches us that we are held by the Spirit that blows where it wills, and we cannot tell where it comes from or where it's going. We only feel it. And we trust that it carries us from God to God. So, by God's grace, we let go . . . and let God. Perhaps we will cling to each other in a love at least as sweet, in a love that will not let us go, even the very fullness of divine love.

My soul clings to you, O God, and your right hand holds me fast.

Church, what do you think? Perhaps it's safe to cross the street now. Shall we go now? I think the way is clear. Death is behind us. Grief cannot define us. Confusion will not keep us. Grave clothes are falling from us even now. A resurrection life awaits us.

By God's grace and to God's glory. Amen.

Easter Sunday, April 16, 2017

Chapter Fourteen

Beyond Our Wants

As a preacher, I prefer obscure texts to the well-worn, familiar texts of the Bible — I don't believe I am alone in that regard. Relatively unfamiliar texts surrender their songs as something new or refreshing. I find it more difficult to clear away the dust of familiarity than to unearth the largely unknown. The Book of Psalms represents a largely untracked landscape in the practice of preaching. Congregations are familiar with the Book of Psalms as responsive readings, or in fragments, or as a part of a liturgy, or sung pieces, but as texts for sermonic explication and application, they are relatively unknown. I couldn't resist that aspect of their unfamiliarity. There was another bonus: while I could say, truthfully, that I was "preaching from the lectionary" I was, in fact, turning in a "get out of lectionary jail card."

Another part of my reasoning goes to the fact that Jesus frequently speaks the psalms when he self-describes; indeed, the Jesus we meet in the gospels favored the Book of Psalms almost above any other book. If we want to know the soul of Jesus, and not only the story, we perhaps need to learn his songs. And that means preaching them . . . or singing them. During a class on preaching the psalms, one of my former students employed this technique, interspersing sermonic speech with sung congregational refrains. With the skilled assistance of our music minister, we collaborated together to create a sermon that moved from speech to song and from song to speech.

This reflects the homiletical process that led to preaching for a season from the Book of Psalms; however, homiletic considerations belie the troubled reality of the City of Baltimore, especially poverty, addiction, racism, and gun violence. I read somewhere that three organizations are still strong in the inner city: gangs, grassroots organizations, and churches (in that order). Included in these church-related efforts is an urban mission-immersion organization which is housed on our campus. Under the wise guidance of pastoral leaders, adolescents from the suburbs or rural areas spend a week in neighborhood congregations, including Sandtown-Winchester, Darley Park, and others.

Participants in these immersion experiences see the scars of the city as well as its hopeful, strong interior. But one Saturday, while participating in a youth event being hosted by a West Baltimore congregation, members of a visiting youth group witnessed one of the 343 killings that took place in Baltimore in 2017. The next day, they joined us for worship. Beginning in April of 2017, our congregation pledged to memorialize each one of those deaths through the year, reading the names of the deceased as a part of our congregational prayer. These prayers were symbolized by purple ribbons, one for each victim, which were taken by members of the congregation as we prayed. After services, the ribbons were tied on the Park Avenue side of the sanctuary.

The youth group sat near the front of the congregation during the worship hour — that had not been the original plan. Apparently, the organizer had intended to bring the group to another church, but because of what they had witnessed, they chose to stay on our campus, where the mission-immersion program is housed, so they could process the experience. At the end of the service, the young people asked if they could take the purple ribbons representing the lives lost that week and bind those to the church wall.

It was as if the ribbons gave them a language with which to express the inexpressible. Perhaps the song of the psalmist did so as well. . . .

Sermon

> *The Lord is my shepherd, I shall not want.*
> *He makes me lie down in green pastures;*
> *he leads me beside still waters;*
> *he restores my soul.*
> *He leads me in right paths for his name's sake.*
> *Even though I walk through the darkest valley,*
> *I fear no evil; for you are with me;*
> *your rod and your staff —*
> *they comfort me.*
> *You prepare a table before me*
> *in the presence of my enemies;*
> *you anoint my head with oil;*
> *my cup overflows.*
> *Surely goodness and mercy shall follow me*
> *all the days of my life,*
> *and I shall dwell in the house of the Lord*
> *my whole life long.*
>
> — Psalm 23

In contrast to the way our psalm begins — "The Lord is my shepherd, I shall not be in want" (1) — our sung refrain turns the noun, "shepherd", into a verb: "*Shepherd* — prod me, guide me, lead me, push me, shove me, O God, beyond my wants, beyond my fears, from death into life." As in, perhaps the composer felt that many of us are still hounded by wants and stalked by fears.

We pray to God; we call God our shepherd; we shall not want. But maybe sometimes we need God to be a verb, to shepherd us, rather than a noun only, our shepherd. Maybe we are aware of the way in which scarcity, or fear, or hunger, or greed nips at our heels; or sometimes the way anxiety will launch itself at us from a shadowy, hidden part of our souls. It happens in the most ordinary places. Standing beside a magazine rack, sometimes the so-called "perfect body" on the cover will lunge at you, snapping at a fragile body image. Or looking at the budget at the end of the month, doing the deadly math, as the numbers count out the relentless advance of poverty, always getting closer — it suffocates laughter, it smothers liberty, makes a mockery of justice. *And it comes quickly*. . . .

Shepherd me, O God, beyond my wants, beyond my fears, from death into life.[47]

It's a perceptive recasting of Psalm 23 and it may lead us to revisit this text, to gain its wisdom for our daily life — where we feel as if we are pursued by wolves of scarcity and roaring lions of greed.

That's not how we usually hear this text, in the heat of the chase. Typically, this psalm serves as the idyllic poem included at the end of life, when all our struggles are done. But apart from that moment, they seem too far removed from our daily existence to merit much practical value. But, over this past week, as I've lived with the Twenty-Third Psalm, I've come to see it in a different light. Maybe this psalm isn't as idyllic and at peace as we initially imagined. And if so, it may teach us something about God's way of keeping us alive.

Consider the verb, *radaph*, translated as "follow" in the NRSV at the end of Psalm 23: "Your goodness and love will *follow* me all the days of my life." Sounds soothing, doesn't it? Like a Bassett Hound, padding along behind you, a dog smile panting with canine affection.

I like Bassett Hounds, but it might be too domesticated for this verse. According to one scholar, we'd be better off translating the Hebrew *radaph* as "pursued" — "God's goodness and love will pursue me all the days of my life." In the larger context of the Book of Psalms, this verb shows up in the

---

[47] Marty Haugen, "Shepherd Me, O God" in *Lift Up Your Hearts: Psalms, Hymns, and Spiritual Songs* (Grand Rapids: Faith Alive Christian Resources, 2013), 456.

settings where the singer is being hunted, stalked, entrapped by an aggressive, and relentless predator:

- "The enemy pursues me and overtakes me" (7:5);
- "[The enemy will] pursue and seize that person whom God has forsaken" (71:11);
- "The wicked . . . pursued the poor and the needy and the brokenhearted to their death" (109:16).[48]

That's the larger context for this verb, to pursue, and it informs how we might hear God's love and goodness — it is in hot pursuit.

How about its immediate context? Try putting Psalm 22 and Psalm 23 together, as if Psalm 23 answers the complaint of Psalm 22: Psalm 22 begins with the complaint: "My God, my God, why have you forsaken me?" Psalm 23 concludes with the assurance: "God's goodness and love will pursue me all the days of my life, and I will dwell in the house of the Lord forever."[49]

If Psalm 23 gives us the sonorous sound of a sheep in an oasis of green pastures and still waters, Psalm 22 bleats with the alarmed voice of the sheep under attack. The psalmic sheep of Psalm 22 faces lions, as they roar, mouth open to devour.

Rescue me, deliver my life from the power of the dog — the dog that pursues.

Shepherd me, O God, beyond my wants, beyond my fears, from death into life.[50]

The sheep of Psalm 23 might still be panting from the chase – but its sense of security is returning.

The psalmist uses the language of animal husbandry but by verse 3, we know we're not talking about the care of animals, but the care of our souls: "He restores my soul." This is the "Sunday morning" exit most of churches will take. But I think it's the wrong exit or at least it's not the only exit. Read closely, and you will see that the text mixes these two things, animal husbandry, which was based in village economics, and the restoration of our souls. Here's a clue: the shepherd metaphor was often used for political figures who were charged with caring for the economics and politics of their

---
[48] J. Clinton McCann, Jr., "The Book of Psalms" in *New Interpreter's Bible*, vol. 4 (Nashville: Abingdon Press, 1996), 768.
[49] McCann, Jr., "The Book of Psalms", 771.
[50] Haugen, "Shepherd Me, O God" in *Lift Up Your Hearts*, 456.

communities. Often, they did a lousy job. Not unlike today. But what is unusual and striking is that the psalmist proclaims the Lord as his shepherd.

No king. No president. No congress. No Federal Reserve. No DOW or NASDAQ. No Consumer Index of Confidence.

The Lord — the Lord provides the politics and the economy that keeps us alive, both body (shelter, meaningful labor, safe neighborhoods) and soul (psychological health, marked by thanksgiving, personal integrity, ethical conduct, and strength to face down adversity). It goes back to the story of the Exodus: God delivers the people of Israel out of a predatory, killing economy into a life-giving promised land.

It's that mixing of business with religion that caught the attention of M. Douglas Meeks, a systematic theologian. Back in the 1990s, he wrote a book entitled, *God the Economist*. And when I came across it, I was intrigued. God the Shepherd, I get. But God the Economist? It might strike us as an odd way of talking. It seems a little too worldly. Alan Greenspan? Adam Smith? God? That's not what Meeks means. God isn't religious about the *Wall Street Journal* or Adam Smith. Instead, in speaking of God as the economist, he names the way religion and economics share a common vocabulary: redemption, debt, trust, savings — all these economic words have a theological root. But we've experienced a dramatic cleavage between the two, as if economists talk reality and ministers talk divinity — ships passing in the night, we seem to speak different languages. But Meeks reminds us that the root of our word economics isn't with Adam Smith but with *oikos*, or household.[51] The picture given to us by Acts is a picture of *oikos*, the household of God: "All who believed were together and had all things in common; they would sell their possessions and goods and distribute the proceeds to all as any had needs" (2:45). Acts gives us a picture of a theological economy — which keeps us alive. So, here's my attempt to paraphrase Psalm 23, with this idea in mind:

The Lord is my Economist. I shall not lack anything.
My Economist makes me lay down in sustainable habitats;
   My Economist leads me to an environmentally protected water supply;
   My Economist keeps me alive by giving me
   a living wage, affordable healthcare, opportunities,
   and a safe place to call home.
My Economist leads me in paths of ethical consumption, for his name's sake.

---

[51] M. Douglas Meeks, *God the Economist: The Doctrine of God and Political Economy* (Minneapolis: Fortress Press, 1989).

Even though I shop and work in the total darkness of modern capitalism,
*   with lions of greed devouring everywhere,*
I will fear nothing.
For you are with me.
Your law and your justice —
they comfort and they guide me.
You prepare the richest budget for me,
Every quarter full of thanksgiving and of song,
whether it is a bowl beans or a festive table loaded
with the finest things,
I rejoice.
In the presence of my enemies,
in the presence of those who would gloat over my failure,
who would say that the market rules,
in their faces,
you prosper me
and my wellness increases.
Truly, my Economist pursues me
with goodness and love for the world.
And I will dwell with the whole household of God —
all God's children —
now and forever. Amen.

That might be the theology of Psalm 23 — Rob Hoch style — but it's too good to leave to theology. Let it form our living, the truest form of theology I know.

So, to begin . . . first, borrowing from Tom Long, this Psalm reminds us that while God may move us, not all that moves us is of God. Wolves of fear and scarcity move us — we run, yelping with fear to the safest neighborhoods. But if God pursues us with love and goodness, it's not so much *where* we go but with *whom* we go that matters. And if you go with God, you go as beloved, not frightened, hungry, forsaken shadows of your true selves.

That changes the dynamic. And it also compels us to discern the source of our movement: are we being moved by a sense of who we are and whose we are? If it's fear of bankruptcy that motivates our utterances and decisions — either as a congregation or as a people — then I would say that the wolf of scarcity has already overtaken us.

God may move us, but not all that moves us is of God — we are sheep of God's fold and we recognize the shepherd's voice because he leads us into life, and life in abundance. Next thing — God doesn't call us to "like" one another but to love one another. That includes enemies — fine in the abstract, in theory, but in this psalm, it's not only an idea; it's a context. We're feasting in the presence of our enemies.

Ellen Charry, an Old Testament scholar, underlines the ambiguity of the preposition, "in the presence of my enemies." Does it mean at a nearby post, where the singer's enemies are watching? Or perhaps the singer eats with his enemies, at the same table? Could it be that their status as enemies has been subverted by the table of God's radical and providential grace?[52]

I'm not sure where I am in terms of "in the presence of my enemies" — there are a lot of churches out there that would like to see First & Franklin fail. They keep predicting it. And they can point to some numbers — mainline liberal congregations are in decline. Including this one. They say you can't celebrate LGBTQ people — you'll die as a congregation. They say you can't love who you were created to love — that's a sin. They want us to fail. They don't believe in our marital politics. They don't believe in a reign of God politics, where God liberates us from killing economies to a living economics.

I want to see us grow but, if I'm honest, part of me also wants to grow *in the presence of our enemies*. Preaching a living wage, affordable healthcare, and a living God *in their faces*. I want to feast at the table of Jesus' inclusive love — and I want them, our enemies, to salivate with envy, I want them to foam at the mouth with their hateful slogans. I'd love to have them come out here one Sunday and picket us with signs and slogans and slurs. And at the end of the service, we'll bring them lemonade and tell them that they are loved by God.

Or . . . it could be, that it means we have been reconciled, that we are being reconciled, that we will be reconciled. That something or *Someone* is moving us beyond our wants, beyond our fears, beyond categories of friend and enemy. Pray for your enemies, bless them and do not curse them, says our Lord Jesus Christ.

Finally, God may not answer all our wants, but God is faithful to give us strength for all our needs.

A pastor had been visiting a member of his church, Anna, who was in the hospital with a terminal diagnosis. During their visits, he would pray; or

---

[52] Ellen Charry, *Sighs and Songs: Psalms 1-50* in the Brazos Theological Commentary on the Bible (Grand Rapids: Brazos Press, 2015), 119.

sometimes she would pray. As time went on, the disease progressed. Her strength began to ebb. And one day, when it came time to pray, she stopped him: "Pastor," she said, "I don't think I'm going to get better. Let's say we skip the prayer for healing today? I just want you to pray for the Lord not to leave me. That's all I need now – the close company of God."

Cancer, hungry as always, overtook her body, but it did not turn her from hope in her redeemer. Her pastor, still a sheep in God's earthly fold, says that she died 25 years ago. Anna's prayer instincts continue to instruct him in his love of God.[53]

As she prayed, so we pray today . . .

Shepherd me, O God, beyond my wants, beyond my fears, from death into life.[54]

Amen.

May 7, 2017

---

[53] Peter W. Marty, "Prayer Without Answers" in *Christian Century* (April 3, 2017) accessed on 4 June 2018 at https://www.christiancentury.org/article/prayer-without-answers.
[54] Haugen, "Shepherd Me, O God" in *Lift Up Your Hearts*, 456.

Chapter Fifteen

Mostly Healthy

I've struggled with depression all of my adult life. It runs in the family, like my blue eyes and (nearly) black hair. Yet, unlike some who struggle with chronic mental illness, I am high functioning, meaning I can usually get out of bed in the morning; make coffee; get dressed; fix the kids their lunch; work productively; laugh at myself; maybe even cheer others up along the way. Others cannot function. We see them living on the streets, in shelters, or just out of sight, a campsite hidden in a copse of trees. Or we don't see them, because they are incarcerated, our criminal justice system criminalizing a common and all too human disability.

Last night, I attended a PTO meeting at the school where our son attends — the topic was mental illness, depression and anxiety disorders, especially in children and adolescents. The presenter, a psychologist, was informative. Among other things, she said clergy were guilty of preaching sermons in which they said things like, "If you're not happy, you need to get 'prayed up'" — she said that we need to educate our clergy. I was glad that I wasn't wearing a collar that evening. Of course, like it or not, she spoke truth. For many congregations, preaching from a psalm is not only dark, it is rare. Venturing to pray the psalms poses risks, too. When I shared with a church member that I was praying the psalms (she knew about my struggle with depression), she looked at me with genuine alarm and asked, "Are you sure that's a good idea? Couldn't you try reading something else, something less dark?"

The North American pulpit has spoon fed the gospel of positive thinking to its churches for so long that many American Christians believe that the lament, the confusion of the psalmist, is a foreign and perhaps even dangerous language. And yet, if the studies are correct, most of us will know some form of mental illness in our lifetimes and all of us know someone who struggles with mental illness.

I discovered the psalmist during one of the loneliest periods of my life, the first six months of ordained ministry. I don't know why I started praying the psalms; maybe it was the way I'd heard others, more experienced in the life of the soul than me, speak of the psalmist, in almost mystical terms, as a companion; it could have been simple desperation. However, it came to pass, I began there, reading one psalm each morning. Usually, I wrote a brief poem, imitating the simplicity of the psalm.

It was the beginning of a journey in prayer in which I acquired a language better than my own, even God's language, for the human experience. Dietrich Bonhoeffer marveled at the psalmist, who gave expression to a great spasm of human feelings (anger, anxiety, loneliness, joy, confusion, hope, peace, disillusionment, trust) while at the same time being God's Word (and, by implication, God's experience). Suddenly, the dark night of the soul, that disturbance within me, was a piece of God's own experience. What is more, I learned from Bonhoeffer to read the psalmist not only for myself, which was not always either desirable or possible (depending on the psalm), but to read the psalmist in an intercessory way, as though Christ breathed through my spirit on behalf of another.

Psalm 31 is not the song of the mostly healthy, high-functioning. But maybe that's the whole point, to supply, as I put it in the sermon, 31-milligrams of psalmic empathy for those who are not mostly healthy. We sing it robustly, as our own song, just as we grieve deeply, though with hope. The faithful are capacitated to sing its confusion by virtue of the whole sweep of the Book of Psalms, almost as if that Book were a "holding place" or a "third space" in which speech is received as a gift, no matter how broken, because it is God's speech . . . or God's own strangled sigh.

Sermon

> *In you, O Lord, I seek refuge,*
> *do not let me ever be put to shame. . . .*
> *Be gracious to me, O Lord,*
> *for I am in distress;*
> *my eye wastes away from grief,*
> *my soul and body also.*
> *For my life is spent with sorrow,*
> *and my years with sighing;*
> *my strength fails because of my misery,*
> *and my bones waste away.*
> *I am the scorn of all my adversaries,*
> *a horror to my neighbors,*
> *an object of dread to my acquaintances;*
> *those who see me in the street flee from me.*
> *I have passed out of mind like one who is dead;*
> *I become like a broken vessel.*
> *For I hear the whispering of many —*
> *terror all around! —*
> *as they scheme together against me, as they plot to take my life.*
> *But I trust in you, O Lord;*
> *I say, "You are my God."*

City Preaching

— Psalm 31:1, 9-14

Our psalmist feels afflicted this morning. He hears whispers of terror all around. A net, he tells us, has been set for him. Our singer cries easily, at the slightest provocation. He feels so alone. Like the way a plastic bag floats on the wind, listless, meaningless as death itself — something to be stepped around or ignored. People, he says, avoid him. But he hears what they say, the gossip. Words have wings, you know, and they fly from our mouth to ears unseen. He knows they avoid him, avoid his eyes. They step around his wheelchair of emotional captivity, steer clear of the dirty blankets of despair which make up his bed.

And perhaps, we would too. We would step around this sorrowful character, should we see or hear him on the street. Like most people (and unlike our psalmist) we manage our emotions, mostly. Like most people, we suppress whispers of delusion, mostly. Like most people, our nightmares happen at night and not in the light of day. Like most people, we are mostly healthy, mostly assured of our place in life, in our neighborhoods, among our friends, and colleagues. Mostly.

Mostly, the whisper of terror never rises much higher than the realm of our subconscious mind. We mask it, successfully enough, behind smiles of optimism and belonging. Today's psalm is for that part of our lives that seems out of control, that refuses to be obedient, that is not staying healthy, not staying wise or successful. If that voice should ever get the upper hand. . . .

Our singer seems to have mostly failed to manage the darker side of the human condition. He or she sings out of that place. She sings amid an experience of deep brokenness. And she sings of a deeper trust. This person, our singer of broken hallelujahs, has limped, or wheeled his way into the middle of our worship service this morning.

Psalm 31 is a visitor to our church. But she is a visitor who preaches. She doesn't sit quietly at the back of the church. She won't come late or leave early, as so often I have seen in this very church. She has come to church today; and she cried from this pulpit a moment ago; she sang with you in the congregation, and she continues to sing — she testifies, she searches her soul, and cries for our God and for her God, and perhaps, with us, she finds God, a sure defense, a trustworthy, rocky crag, a strong fortress.

Mostly, we would step around this tragic figure — or suggest she see a therapist or encourage her to stay on her meds — and that might not be a bad idea, but today, before we euthanize her with cheap psychology, we will sing with her — she will not receive our meds, but she, through her song, will be medicine for us, because she has joined us in our worship today as God's word sung to us . . .

In you, O Lord, in you have I taken refuge.[55]

Yes, there are a few bright moments, where the clouds of despond break with the bright light of hope: "God," she says, "is my rock, my crag, my sure foundation, my refuge." But we might be more taken by the jig-saw-puzzle–with-a-couple-of-pieces-gone feeling of today's song. If you look at the psalm, it doesn't follow a logical pattern — the first part of the psalm speaks of God as the psalmist's rocky crag, her sure foundation. A refuge, a sanctuary, a place of deep security. But by verse 4, we hear the worried, almost paranoid outburst from the back pew of doubt: "They've set a net for me, to trap me; I hear whispers of terror all around." Verse 9-13, the psalmist shifts from persecution, perhaps to emotional exhaustion and physical illness:

> "My years pass in sighs; my eyes melt with tears. My bones melt, and I am sick to my stomach. I am like the dead, my body discarded, left in a landfill while the rest of the world rages with progress."

At the same time, you hear among these laments, deep expressions of trust:

> "I commit my spirit to you. My spirit, my life is in your hands O God."

What do you with a text like this? Complain, among other things. Scholars *complain* when texts don't proceed in a coherent manner. Often, they want the *theory of the psalm* rather than the *psalm itself*. They grouse about the incoherent jumbling of genres, lament and praise; a chaotic fruit salad of confidence and despair.

One reader "gerrymanders" the text in order to help it make sense — the term comes from the political realm, where politicians redraw the boundaries of the district to exclude neighborhoods that would likely oppose their candidacy.

So, in order to make this text into a friendly district of theological coherence, she gerrymandered the text, drawing a weird loop around verses that made coherent sense together on their own, while at the same time excluding those

---

[55] Hal H. Hopson, "Psalm 31" in *The Psalter: Psalms & Canticles for Singing* (Louisville: Westminster/John Knox Press, 1993), 28.

that did not, essentially segregating the lament to one side of the psalmic neighborhood — where life was crap — and keeping the happy healthy congregation in a theologically privileged neighborhood, where life was mostly pretty good. All so it would make sense. Finally, I came across another reader who just gave up and said, essentially, "You know, this is the way broken people talk; this is the way hurting people pray; this is the way grieving people sing."[56]

That's where I landed with the illogic of this psalm: it's a broken hallelujah!

But a broken hallelujah, even if it's broken, it is a hallelujah still. In Luke's gospel, Christ himself takes this song as his own as he is dying, part sigh and part proclamation (Luke 24:36). The brokenness of Jesus' death on the cross does not cancel out faithful proclamation. So, also, Stephen, as he is dying, a religious mob preparing to lynch him, takes this very text, verse 59 of today's reading from Acts, onto his lips: "I commit my spirit into your hands, my life into your care" (Acts 7:59). There is, however, a difference between the way Christ prays this psalm and the way the psalmist prays. Ellen Charry points out that Christ prays this psalm as he is dying, just as Stephen does. His suffering is great, but it is not life-long. The psalmist pours out his years in sighs. She sees another difference: the psalmist isn't an innocent martyr. Our singer is a sinner *and* he is sinned against. Think King David — he sinned, murdered Uriah the husband of Bathsheba. He sinned. Visibly. But he is also sinned against — and today's psalm gives speech to that experience.[57]

Charry suggests that as we read this psalm, we read it through the lens of someone who goes to prison in his younger years. Maybe he is an African-American. Maybe he committed a crime — a real crime with a real victim. He sinned. While in prison, he lives in an environment that victimizes again. He was sinned against. Prisons purport to be rehabilitative but at least as often they are just plain retributive, dealing out pain in the name of justice. Wounded people are wounded all over again — this time in the name of justice.

For his work, he is perhaps paid $30 a month, wages that would be considered slavery outside of prison walls. Medical care is scant or non-existent. AIDS HIV rampant. Loneliness is killing. Our prisoner doesn't expect birthday cards from the victims of his crime. But he doesn't hear from his family either, or his father, or perhaps even his friends. No one speaks of him or even to him. He is forgotten. It's as if he died while in prison. Or that

---

[56] McCann, Jr., "The Book of Psalms" in *New Interpreter's Bible*, vol. 4, 799.
[57] Charry, *Sighs and Songs of Israel*, 157.

he lives in a city of populated with the groans and miseries of dead people.[58] Amid those groans, he learns to sing a different song, a song in which he flies to a place of security and confidence . . .

In you, O Lord, in you have I taken refuge.[59]

In the city of the dead, a manmade necropolis, our prisoner finds security, a rocky crag of God's trustworthiness. And that song gives him strength, no matter his circumstances. But then, lo and behold, he is released. But is he ever released, released from the prison his neighbors make for him as a so-called "free" man? Released to a halfway house, he goes out for a run. It's a cold, drizzly day. He looks odd in a t-shirt and shorts. A police officer waves him over. He complies, as obedient as a child. The police officer asks, "What are you doing out here dressed like that?"

"What do you mean dressed like that? This is what I wear to jog."

The officer looks him up and down, skeptical. "Where's your identification?"

"I don't have any on me," he says, "I'm going for a jog."

"Really? Where are you from?"

"I'm staying at the halfway house, up there. I just got out of prison."

"How long were you in prison?"

"A long time," he says.

"How long?" he asks. "Ten years?"

"More than ten years," he answers.

"Fifteen years?"

"More than fifteen years."

"Twenty years?"

"More than twenty years."

---

[58] Charry, *Sighs and Songs of Israel*, 158-61.
[59] Hopson, "Psalm 31" in *The Psalter*, 28.

"How many years?"

"Nearly forty years, officer."

"Well, now," he says to him, "you must be a real piece of [expletive]. I don't want to see you here again. You get back to that halfway house and you don't come out again until you have identification."

"Yes, sir," he says.

A man who has paid his dues to society, he lives on both sides of the street — as sinner but also as one who is sinned against.

Maybe he knows this prayer better than those of us who mostly manage to keep our lives under control. Who mostly manage to fit into a gerrymandered world, where our neighbors are mostly like us, mostly successful, mostly happy, mostly honest, mostly well-regarded. Mostly coherent. Except perhaps for those parts of our life that are not . . . feelings of anxiety that we cannot tame; imagined whispers of scorn; the well-spring of self-loathing that sometimes grows in us.

And we find we can sing with our visitor who is more like a fellow pilgrim than a stranger. So, what shall we do with this psalm which has so rudely intruded into our gerrymandered world?

Perhaps its word reminds us that God in Christ comes to make the captive free, the lame walk, the lost found — and when you're that kind of person, we like to celebrate: "I was lost but now I'm found!" I don't want to get in the way of that. But if you've been lost, if you've experienced disability, if you've been a captive, you never quite forget the experience. That's God's language, too.

And that God slips into our vocabulary — the language of the captive, of the unstable. We speak the language of God's faithfulness, of God's dependability. But we do not speak to exclude those who struggle, and gasp, and sob for their hallelujahs.

Our psalm today softens us to those in our midst who maybe cannot speak coherently — whose actual lives don't conform to the theoretical life: go to college, get a job, get married, and enjoy a postcard perfect retirement. Today, we get 31-milligrams of psalmic empathy. But perhaps one of the side effects of that psalmic medicine: that side effect allows us to name those parts of our lives that are *not* mostly okay. Where we know that we feel shame. We feel bullied. We feel overwhelmed. Or we fear being outed — or we have been outed but every outing terrifies us, makes us sick to our stomach.

That place in you belongs to God as much as your praise belongs. That hurt belongs to God. Before it was your hurt, it was God's hurt.

Before we grieved, God grieved for us. Before we loved God, God first loved us. God remains faithful, dependable. A rocky crag. Our fortress in the shifting sands of circumstance.

Finally, the psalmist sings and testifies in our congregation — she knows us as her neighbors. Her song prods us to reflect on how we will behave — her neighbors and her congregation — when we see her, disheveled, when we her hear, saying, God bless you through the fog of a debilitating addiction, and all the shame and self-loathing she must feel. Will we respond like the neighbors responded to the psalmist? Will we avert our eyes? Or will we be moved to care?[60]

As I said, the visitor to our church today, Psalm 31, she brings medicine. She gives us the medicine of empathy. The powers of the world are committed to gerrymandering our society: Dump the sick population into the pools of even sicker populations. Keep the healthy with the healthy. And let the groaning weep in the prisons of their own making . . . or our making.

While we sing our happy hallelujahs . . .

But today, she insists, she sings. Today he sweats in a fever of fear and faith. Today she testifies with unusual confidence and startling honesty about the goodness of God.

Today she proclaims her trust in God, in this congregation, in neighbors who dare to care. Let us sing with her — and let us sing with Christ. . . .

In you, O Lord, in you have I taken refuge.[61]

Amen.

May 14, 2017

---

[60] Charry, *Sighs and Songs of Israel*, 164.
[61] Hopson, "Psalm 31" in *The Psalter*, 28.

Chapter Sixteen

Seven Years Old

– Inspired by the Story of Jacob and Rebekah

I'm not sure what triggered this sermon, which is only loosely connected to the story of Jacob and Rebekah. Maybe it's the way the writer of Genesis puts it: the first seven years that Jacob worked for Rebekah passed as if they were a dream, he was so in love. But the second seven years — that was a different story!

When I wrote this sermon, Gabriel had been pestering us about when his next birthday, his seventh birthday, would arrive. He actually exhausted us with the question, it seemed like several times a day: "When's my birthday? How long is it from now? How many days is that?" and so on.

I got to the point that I would hang my head and sigh, "I'm not sure Gabriel, more than a few weeks." And, of course, that never satisfied.

Perhaps, then, it was a form of frustration that gave birth to this sermon (that gives birth to every sermon!). Additionally, it was, in some sense, a welcome (if somewhat guilty) relief from close textual interpretation. It gave me permission to engage in the poetry of preaching, in its personal dimension. It was a children's sermon, but at a slant, with the whole congregation invited to consider the whole of life, love, experience, loss as a witness to the gift of life itself. So, in love, so deeply in love, life passes through us as if it were a dream. And yet, we know, too, that our lives consist of difficulty, of hopes unrealized, of days cut short — and these days seem to be long and dry. So that was the sermon.

My lasting memory will be of Gabriel in the pew, or rather, the picture of Gabriel popping up from his mother's lap each time I spoke his name. At least once, he blushed with the thought that he might love someone as much as his mother. As I write, in the month of April, he is asking again about his birthday. He can't wait. . . .

Sermon

> *So Jacob served seven years for Rachel, and they seemed to him but a few days because of the love he had for her.*
>
> — *Genesis 29:20*

Gabriel, our six-year-old, counts the days to his next birthday — he has been doing so for the last six months or so. "When's my birthday?" he asks.

"In August," comes our reply.

"How long is that?" he asks.

"A long time," we say.

"How many days?" he asks.

Then we do the math . . . and actually, Gabriel, you have just 30 days until your next birthday. Thirty days. Thirty *long* days

But I assure you, Gabriel, that these days, though they seem long, will pass more and more quickly as you age. When you get to my age, days will slip by like snowflakes falling to the ground, or like leaves slipping from their lofty heights in the fall; when you get to my age, you will wonder where all the time went; you will wonder, "When did my parents turn grey and feeble?"; you will wonder at your own eyes, the crow's feet there, which you had never seen before; you will see your days and you will see how fast, how quickly they go. And you will begin to number your days. . . .

But not now. You'll be too busy to count — you will sprint through your youth, as if it would last forever, you will jump on the bicycle of experience, lower yourself over the handlebars of existence and you will fly, the wind catching your hair, you will feel the rush of experience roaring in your ears, you will feel your own strength, your arms muscled, sinewy and lean, your passion feverish and intense; you will fall in love one day, Gabriel . . . .

I know you don't think it will happen, you say, "Not me" but it will, you will. The one you love will fill your thoughts and your dreams. You will almost forget your mother, almost. The one you love — time then will be so deep, so lasting. You will never forget the first electric moment when your lips touched, or that moment when your hands brushed together, finger tips first, and a spasm of wonder swept through you. If you so love, as I hope you will love one day, it may be only a moment, but it will hold a thousand years in a single memory.

Or it may be that your experience of love will be so powerful that all the years of waiting will be like a few days, like a few moments of breathless anticipation, as you take a breath, preparing to make a wish. . . .

Perhaps you will not regret the long days waiting. They will seem but a moment, barely a thought. But there may be other days in your life which are, indeed, long, dry, repeating.

Right now, days are long because you are more future than memory. You open your eyes in the morning to a world pregnant with nearly limitless possibility. But there comes a time in all of our lives when we are more memory than future. One day, you will open your eyes and you will remember what you loved, who you loved, by whom you were loved.

You will see us, perhaps, your family somewhere in the tableau of recollection. Perhaps you will see the people of this church. I hope what you see will bring you happiness. But Gabriel, even though I would take it from you if I could, you will, by God's terrible grace, know days that are long with sorrows, too. Grief, I have heard it said, is the tax we pay for loving people. Love, someone said, is a kind of poison. Happiness, someone wrote, isn't a place where you live forever but an apartment where the rent isn't stabilized, much less controlled.

Love, joy, happiness — fickle things, here today and gone tomorrow. Human love includes its animal passions, its internal contradictions, its blindness, its disdain, its jealousies, its betrayals, its cravings and its fears. . . . When the days become long, when love feels like a poison, or when happiness is the address of your eviction, because of poverty, because of heartbreak, because of disease, because of failure, because of disappointment, because we are thrown into circumstances that we did not choose, or we could not evade, when that day comes, if that day comes, do not forsake love, true love, even though the day seems long.

Some will tell you to let love go. Submit to the edicts of humanistic reason. Wed yourself to a deflationary skepticism. . . . But Scripture says something else — says that God's love and our love for God is this crazy affirmation of something greater than our sorrows. It affirms that our tears will turn to songs of happiness; it cries out that sorrow may spend the night, but joy will come in the morning. We may grieve, this people of God, but we do not grieve as others grieve, as people without hope. We grieve more *because* we hope. We grieve hot tears *because* we have seen Jesus, living God, in our midst. And we grieve with the longing of the lover who calls for her beloved, and she will not be comforted until her children who are no more are restored to her arms.

Listen to her, Gabriel, listen to her unreasonable grief — she will not be comforted, her secret heart will not be comforted apart from the hand, the voice, the breath of the beloved for whom she longs. Days like these seem long — too long. Like the addict who counts the days in sobriety, even as he regrets the irreparable wounds of the addiction. Or like me, counting the days of a passing middle age. Or counting the days lost in work, decades of work that does not dignify, that does not lend meaning, that does not lift up. Counting the hours, from 9 to 5, and knowing what you take home will never make a home.

Gabriel, son of God, child of the covenant, sometimes love, hope, joy — they seem like poison, like they perhaps make us sick, craving it so deeply that, in its absence, we imagine we would be healthier without it, more balanced if we were untouched by love's poison. If you did not love, Gabriel, it is true, if you did not love, you might not suffer, at least not over much. You might not grieve, at least not immodestly. You would not care with passionate intensity — you might read the newspaper, cast your vote, become a churchgoer, but you would not stand with the bodies of the oppressed. If you did not love. You would not seek wisdom but simply acquire knowledge. If you did not love, a degree would suffice. An ironic wink and a cynical outlook would pass for intelligence. A specialization would be enough. Savings for a fearful retirement, without love. You would simply get on with life so as to minimize suffering. Moderate your emotions. Self-medicate with consumerist addictions. And people will praise you for what they call, balance.

But, Gabriel, if you love, as God loves, you will know the immoderate, ravishing, and extravagant gift of God's presence in our days — our days messy with God's love. I love you more than I can say. I feel like a thousand years some mornings, tousling your hair. Like I was looking into a telescope of being seeing more than I can know. More than my feeble heart can stand, even. And I don't know the years that the good Lord has given me to share with you.

Your future or mine — I cannot see it. I crave it and I fear it.

And I confess that sometimes, I complain, the days seem long. The future, what it brings or does not bring, I try to predict. What it denies, I try to seize. I forge truces and alliances; I sign contracts of agreement, of remuneration and release — in this hour, in this place, with this people, under the gaze of worldly powers. Sometimes, I'm like a drunk driver, swerving with depression, drifting with false loves — false loves from which I try to gain advantage or security, false loves which seem easier than true love; false love that prefers one and neglects the other.

And they — everyone around you, Gabriel — they're doing the same. False loves wage a war for our loyalty, for our hearts, for our very souls. And we, all of us, to a one, succumb to the temptation of false loves.

But by God's grace, by the quickening of the Spirit within us, the secret voice within us stirs up a hunger for a future that we cannot know. By God's grace, we too desire a vision for living greater than the simple passing of days, efficient and bloodless. And none of us, Gabriel, not me, not anyone, knows how to handle the One who is coming.

For it is not our false loves that rise up to meet us this day and every day — not our strategies, our alliances, our contracts, our worldly success, or selfish ambitions — these false loves pale in comparison to the One who comes to us, the One who finally holds us fast, both in our living and in our dying, this One comes. Because, we believe, we confess that the One who is coming at every moment, the One through whom every breath becomes song, in whom every breath becomes air — and by whom lifeless air becomes living breath — this One comes, like the darkness of glory, like the breathlessness of awe, like the wonder of new creation.

God is love. With true love, our hands always tremble. With love, our nervous reason quiets itself, like an infant at her mother's breast. With love, we are vulnerable to machinations of others. But with love, we dare to live. But with love, we dare to die.

But with love. . . .

We are dysfunctional all the way. You'll probably need counseling, to work out your issues with mom and dad. Yet, amid this stuff — our betrayals and our blindness, our contracts and competition — God begins anew. Love again. Love renewed. Love remaking. Unreasonable, often. But steadfast, God elects this funky family as God's own family — messy, and God, fully like us, or the perfect image within us, opening to us God's future. . . . A future in which our sicknesses are healed, where our cravings are satisfied, where our alienation is overcome, where expected shame becomes unexpected honor.

Gabriel, it's just 30 days until your birthday. But who's counting, right? May that day be renewed then, and now, and for as long as we both shall live. And longer. May it be so for all of us. Until Christ comes again.

Amen.

July 30, 2017

Chapter Seventeen

Learning a New Song

Ordination sermons bring me close to that space I occupied as a seminary professor; that is, somewhere in that space between classroom and sanctuary. At the time of this sermon, I had left the University of Dubuque Theological Seminary about a year before. Tamara, who was my advisee while I was there, transferred to a different seminary, where she completed her degree. Even though neither of us were any longer affiliated with the seminary where we met, it felt a bit like seminary again, only better.

What makes an ordination sermon different from a typical Sunday morning sermon? Ordination sermons are topical sermons rather than strictly textual (as are most of the sermons in this collection). An ordination sermon explores the broad and deep themes of call and response. It is rooted in the theology of baptism, covenant, and discipleship.

For ministers, the ordination service represents an "inflection point" in the ministerial vocation. In Reformed theology, ordination is a footnote to one's baptism. At the same time, it is triumphant, like the moment when the bride and groom meet at the front of the church, preparing to say their vows. The aisle stands as a parable that leads to covenant promise. You could also say that it marks the beginning of one's "daily" vocation in parish ministry. The ordinand designs the service, from beginning to end. It is actually quite a feat, like herding cats, to get everyone to the same place at the same time, playing their parts. Tamara excelled in this regard, suggestive of a bright future in parish ministry!

Recently, I read an article by an Australian writer who says that he writes with his heart in his mouth — it sounds like something a preacher would say. Or actually, something a preacher-poet, George Herbert, did say: ". . . By dipping and seasoning all our words and sentences in our hearts before they come into our mouths, truly affecting and cordially expressing all that we say, so that the auditors may plainly perceive that every word is heart-deep."[62] While he wrote about all preaching, his wisdom is especially appropriate for an ordination sermon. Pastorally, for congregations, the sermon might be

---

[62] Herbert, *The Temple and the Country Parson* (Boston: James B. Dow, 1842 [1652]), excerpted in Lischer, ed., *The Company of Preachers*, 66.

something like reading an affectionate preface written by a friend of the author of a book that is yet to be discovered, a story yet to be told.

Sermon

> *But Moses said to the Lord, "O my Lord, I have never been eloquent, neither in the past nor even now that you have spoken to your servant; but I am slow of speech and slow of tongue." Then the Lord said to him, "Who gives speech to mortals? Who makes them mute or deaf, seeing or blind? Is it not I, the Lord?"*
>
> *Exodus 4:10-11*

Over the last six months or so, I've been meeting with a young person. I'll call him Thomas. And maybe you'll understand my choice of names after you hear some of his story. But please don't think I mean in it a disparaging way, as poor doubting Thomas. I mean it differently.

Thomas is an almost new Christian. Going to baptized in just a few weeks — a different kind of ordination, but no less significant, or in fact at the very heart of what we're about today.

Thomas would strike you, I think, as conscientious, intelligent, thoughtful. He would impress you as a person who, once he has a plan, diligently pursues it. But in the fall of last year, his life took a dramatic detour. He developed a serious throat infection, which required emergency surgery. For any other person, it would have perhaps been routine. But he wasn't an ordinary person. He was a trumpet player. And he was devastated when the surgeon told him that he would not be able to play professionally, a life-long dream. He might not be able to play at all.

But under the circumstances, he had no choice.

He underwent surgery — it probably saved his life, but the life that was saved is at loose ends today. He had been enrolled in a respected music conservatory, with an ambition (and the ability) to play at concert level. That's no longer an option for Thomas. But he tells me that it's more than just the instrument. He could live without the professional career. It's what this instrument symbolized for him. He said that playing the trumpet gave him a place to go, an escape from economic hardship and an abusive father when he was a teen. Through that difficult season, it seemed as if playing the trumpet had given him not only relief but vocation, not only an escape but a competency of which he was rightly proud. Today, he says, he can play for maybe twenty minutes — once a week — and the pain tells him that if he plays any longer, he will only injure himself further. Now, that instrument, which was almost an extension of his body, is mostly useless, sitting in the corner of his small studio apartment.

Where do I go from here? What do you do, he seems to ask, when the instrument you've learned to play, which gave you strength and confidence, even became part of your identity, has been taken away from you?

What do *you* do? What do we do when what seems like our north star and our rising sun, what seems like our perfect path dissolves or disappears or perhaps never was to begin with? Is it the beginning of the end or is the end a new beginning?

Monet, the impressionist, slowly went blind and it seems as if blindness gave him insight that he could not have captured with natural sight. But I wonder if he felt a bit like Thomas, when it dawned on him that something was wrong. Dawned on him that the flowers in his garden were not quite so distinct as they were the day before. Beethoven was practically deaf when he composed his music. But I wonder if, as the birdsong grew more faint each morning, I wonder if he doubted, if he questioned, if he objected. Jacob journeyed down to Egypt, crippled by a blessing, undergoing a transformation from man into nation — but I wonder if, that morning, when he woke up with that wrenched hip, when he limped into the long day of a future he could not see, I wonder if it felt more like an ending than a beginning.

This felt weakness is something that our texts, especially the call narratives of Moses and Jeremiah, attest to — and we could probably follow it into the New Testament, too. The disciples dropped their nets, left boats, and parents — and followed Jesus. Nets and bewildered parents on the lakeshore behind them, maybe it was an ending. But what kind of beginning? What sort of journey?

Across Scripture, it seems as if our willingness to be irrelevant, or an odd duck — a blind painter, or a stuttering orator, or a crippled pilgrim — points to one of the symptoms of faithful response. That is, finding within us a strength not our own, but finding God who becomes the strength for our living, the sure foundation of vocation.

All of us, including yours truly — a once-upon-a-time seminary professor — learned to play a certain kind of instrument — derived strength from it, even meaning and perhaps refuge. We played beautifully. Graduated. Adjusted after setbacks. Prevailed in the midst of adversity. Learned some things along the way. Got tenure. They said of us, how you have matured! How you have grown! They spoke well of us. But perhaps, if this is God's call, if our lives belong to God, perhaps we, too, have undergone an emergency operation — God's salvation operation, which has put us into a bit of a tail spin. It's different for all of us, I suppose. But it happens. God steps into our lives. Teaches a new song. Maybe suddenly it seems as if we can't play the beloved instrument — or, maybe it's this: maybe we could play it, but that instrument can no longer carry notes of the new song of our soul.

Come follow me, and I will make you into fishers of people. Jesus' calling may use the language of instrumentality — a profession, a net, some tools, a bit of training, a set of competencies — but the response suggests not a transaction between inputs and outputs, but a transformation, between God and the human being.

I will *make* you, says Jesus.

The Greek for "make" goes beyond "manufacture" — it suggests creation or formation. It is, in fact, the word from which we get poem, or poetry. God makes us into poems. What can that possibly mean? Do we rhyme? Am I a haiku? Not exactly. Not that kind of poem. God makes us into a people who live at a deeper level than ordinary speech, or ordinary skill, or commonplace competencies can plumb. Poetry, good poetry, exhibits a capacity for irony, or angularity, for seeing and telling the truth slant, as Emily Dickenson puts it. Learning God's song we learn more deeply that we are fearfully and wonderfully made. We seem like ordinary flesh and bone, and yet if we had eyes to see, all of us would seem like pillars of smoke and fire. . . . God didn't aim to introduce a subject but to form a people who burn with holy fire.

The prophet Jeremiah rightly understood that he was not ready — he counted the cost of discipleship, he searched his skills and his knowledge. And he knew the report: insufficient funds. Moses, too, understood that his skillset was better matched to a quiet life, herding his father-in-law's goats than it was speaking truth to power. With a stutter, and a felony on his record, he knew better.

But nevertheless, she persisted. Nevertheless, she persisted. Nevertheless. Our God persists, despite objections, from the world, or anywhere else, including our own.

Our occasion today, Rev. Tamara Razanno's ordination (has a nice ring to it, don't you think?) brought to mind, Henri Nouwen's *In the Name of Jesus*. I'm sure some of you are familiar with it. He wrote it in 1989, almost thirty years ago now, but it still speaks today, in 2017. In it, he chronicles what it felt like to leave Harvard — where his skills as a writer and a mystic, and a leader in the ecumenical movement had a place, a location, and how he left to join an intentional community of people who live with disabilities, a L'Arche community, in Toronto, Canada, where his many skills were irrelevant to his belonging. He could write books, but what was that to people who could not read? He was cosmopolitan, but what was that to this community, a people for whom the world was this little house, the relationships formed around its table, which was set with ordinary food, its life governed by the daily routine of a small family?

Essentially, he reflects on the move from a transactional response to call — in which we determine inputs and outputs — to a more transformational model, in which we are vulnerable, open to the future God is bringing to us. A future which God brings to us, in spite of our best efforts. A calling in which God supplies strength for our needs. By definition, this dynamic, shifting from a transactional relationship to a transformational one, imperils the whole question of our relevance.

This is Nouwen's first, and according to him, most important insight. Relevance is the instrument thrust into our hands from a young age onwards. And we seek to be relevant. We're surrounded by relevant people, who prove their value by doing useful things — doctors administer medicine wisely; mechanics repair carburetors, skillfully; specialists give informed diagnoses of complex problems, dispassionately. Ministers, too, can be swept up in the constant buzz of many things — to do, to complete, to exact, to balance in congregational life. And of these things, there is no end. . . . [63]

I don't live in a L'Arche community like Nouwen. My path isn't identical to Nouwen's. For one, I didn't leave Harvard — I left a small seminary in the Midwest. And I didn't join a small, intentional community. I took a call to an urban congregation, in the heart of downtown Baltimore. So there are differences. But this week, I was on the phone trying to form a human chain of care for one of our members, a man who spent 38-years of his life in prison. In his seventies, he just got a knee replaced. Tattoos of spider webs extend up and down his arms and torso — these suggest deeper scars than the one he has on his knee. But there's a part of him that is proud of those

---

[63] Henri J. M. Nouwen, *In the Name of Jesus* (New York: The Crossroad Publishing Company, 1989), 15-20.

markings, like he was proud of his service to the U.S. Marine Corps during Vietnam. When I let my chin-hair grow, he smiles and says, "You're a rebel" — I guess he knows the kind! He tells me he was a bad, angry dude when he came back from Vietnam. A member of a motorcycle gang, he was an accessory to murder. But the tattoos, even the baseball cap, signify an old life, the memory of the old man, but it's the new man in Christ — he's the one that I know.

He doesn't know the books I've written. Or the books I would like to write. His idea of a defense has nothing to do with a dissertation. I sometimes wonder what he thinks of this preacher dude, with my preacher tattoos. . . .

A professor once asked me to think about what happens to the preacher once she steps out of the pulpit — it's an interesting question. I've never quite solved it. Perhaps, we cease to be *The Preacher*. Or perhaps we never were. Or we were, but only at a slant. Or perhaps, when the preacher leaves her pulpit, the sermon begins in a new form, in the quiet, not quite soaring work of ministry. You remember to bring a cold drink for some of the heroin addicts you know you'll see on your walk to the church. It's not easy to do, really. I forget ten times for every one time I remember, but those moments suggest to me that perhaps I'm beginning to learn servanthood, albeit slowly.

Ministry is quiet, unassuming. But preach we do, like it or not. The preacher speaks. She exists under that solemn obligation. She rises from the pew . . . and she will return to it, as student not master. As fellow sojourner.

I think this ethos leaves a mark on our preaching life. Tamara, don't you think so? We preach less for a glorious ending, but for a faithful beginning — sermons end well when they leave something unfinished, or the spirit unsettled. Something left to be said, or some vision in the night that almost feels like it's part of the dawn of a new day, almost . . . it will take someone willing to receive it, walk into it.

Tamara, you have skills. So do I. I still love the library. And I love the classroom. You can take the professor out of the classroom. . . . A member of our little community e-mailed me this week. He was complaining: "Why is it that the prelude begins at 10:20 a.m. rather than at 10:30 a.m.? Shouldn't the service begin at 10:30 a.m.? Am I the only one who thinks this???" Ending with three question marks accentuated his point, I guess. And in my reply, which I had imagined at first to be sharp and biting, my better angels won out, and I proceeded to give an introductory lecture — which was both objective, clarifying, and beautiful — on the place of preludes in the Reformed Tradition of Christian worship.

That lecture, I delivered it so well. "Where is it now?" you ask. It's over there in the corner. Truth is, I don't play it often. I am a learning a new song. Singing with an old convict. Teaching *somewhat* willing students. Limping into a new day, a future that I do not know. But limping with a God I trust. May it be so for all of us, for Tamara, for the church she serves . . . and for Thomas, too. Say a prayer for Thomas.

Amen.

Ordination of Tamara Razzano
Cooperstown, NY
August 27, 2017

Chapter Eighteen

Ready for Christmas?

Christmas Eve fell on a Sunday this year. And the question I kept hearing and probably asked a few times was, "Are you ready for Christmas?" We know what we mean by that question: we're getting ready for the cultural event called Christmas. But when I thought about how unready the world seemed when Jesus was born — that there was no room for his family at the inn — I heard that question again, only now in a different and more theological and, indeed, national dimension.

We usually preach personal sermons — we tell stories about ourselves, we address the actual congregation, we speak to an identity that might be defined by the congregation. The sermon title (and the occasion) might have suggested a personal direction. But for this sermon, I chose instead to speak to a corporate entity, America. I didn't invent this method of address. Read the prophets and you will find them speaking to their country, to their beloved Israel, to the nation of Judah, or to the nations. There are also echoes of Alan Paton's book, *Cry, the Beloved Country*, a book which moved me deeply when I first read it. Given the violence of our age, I addressed this sermon to a collective identity, namely the United States, or, as I put it in this sermon, America. I was addressing our soul as a nation. While First & Franklin's historical legacy lends itself to this kind of preaching, preachers should consider the personification of our national identity. It's not without its problems. Not everyone in the church is an American, for one. And the idea of the United States being synonymous with America is problematic. At the same time, thinking of the congregation as discreet individuals isn't without its problems either. By evoking a corporate identity, I was able to track the patterns of our own complicity in obeying the decrees of the emperor.

It is no use denying it. All of us are swept up by principalities and powers, just as Joseph and Mary were swept up by the decrees of empire. The text does not, however, endorse mindless fate as our sad destiny. Instead, the generic command yields to the quite specific event of Christ's incarnation as a child born to a young woman named Mary. Ordinary people, even stars and angels, turn their eyes and their songs to this unusual child which has been laid in a manger. In Matthew, the kings of this world hear of the birth of a harmless child to refugee parents and they are afraid.

Maybe I was thinking of Matthew's Massacre of the Infants (Matthew 2:16-18) as much as I was Luke's account of the nativity. By the end of the year,

Baltimore had more killings per capita than any other large city in the United States. Perhaps the insight of Jesus' untimely birth, in an unlikely place, for an unpromising people should interrupt our cheap pleasures with the sharp stab of real grief even as we anticipate the substantive gospel of God's heavenly rule.

Sermon

> *In those days a decree went out from Emperor Augustus that all the world should be registered. This was the first registration and was taken while Quirinius was governor of Syria. All went to their own towns to be registered.*
>
> *Joseph also went from the town of Nazareth in Galilee to Judea, to the city of David called Bethlehem, because he was descended from the house and family of David. He went to be registered with Mary, to whom he was engaged and who was expecting a child. While they were there, the time came for her to deliver her child. And she gave birth to her firstborn son and wrapped him in bands of cloth, and laid him in a manger, because there was no place for them in the inn.*
>
> *In that region there were shepherds living in the fields, keeping watch over their flock by night. Then an angel of the Lord stood before them, and the glory of the Lord shone around them, and they were terrified. But the angel said to them, "Do not be afraid; for see — I am bringing you good news of great joy for all the people: to you is born this day in the city of David a Savior, who is the Messiah, the Lord. This will be a sign for you: you will find a child wrapped in bands of cloth and lying in a manger." And suddenly there was with the angel a multitude of the heavenly host, praising God and saying,*
>
>> *"Glory to God in the highest heaven,*
>> *and on earth peace among those whom he favors!"*
>
> *When the angels had left them and gone into heaven, the shepherds said to one another, "Let us go now to Bethlehem and see this thing that has taken place, which the Lord has made known to us." So they went with haste and found Mary and Joseph, and the child lying in the manger. When they saw this, they made known what had been told them about this child; and all who heard it were amazed at what the shepherds told them. But Mary treasured all these words and pondered them in her heart. The shepherds returned, glorifying and praising God for all they had heard and seen, as it had been told them.*

— Luke 2:1-20

Are you ready for Christmas? Are we ready for Christmas, America? I'm not sure we are. When Donald Trump promised to make America great again, we put him in the White House. But when Jesus came proclaiming good news to the poor, freedom to the captive, light for those who dwell in darkness; when Jesus came to make America *loving* again, we put him in a feeding trough. *A feeding trough.* A place where we throw away the brown ends of carrots, the peelings of potatoes; the place where we toss slop for pigs, and rats, and bones for dogs to fight over; that's where the world put Jesus when he was born.

America, we were ready to make our nation great again. But I don't think we're ready for Christmas.

Maybe that's okay. Mary and Joseph were not ready. Luke gives us a picture of a God born on the road. Even the angels, *the angels* who should know what's happening and when, they weren't ready. Did you notice that? They weren't in the animal stall, where they should have been hovering above the shoulders of the holy family, they were in a field, nearby. They appeared to some shepherds there and announced that this thing had happened.

My guess is that they had been traveling at the speed of theological light, for hundreds if not millions or billions of years in a rush to get to the birthing suite for God, but then their stardust fuel ran out, their engine choked and sputtered, just above these shepherds and since they couldn't go any farther, they told them. And shepherds, well, it was their workday. It was third shift, and they were no way ready for Christmas. The night was half spent, and there was a long night yet to go.

Rome wasn't ready. Emperor Augustus was signing executive orders that all the world should be registered — he wasn't ready for a new kind of rule breaking into his kleptocracy, certainly not from the likes of two immigrant parents.

America, you know this, in your heart you know it. We're not ready; I'm not ready; we're not ready for Christ's real presence. And this morning, I would love to say to you that America is ready, but if I did so, it would be false. It's got its lights and its trees. Corporations are meeting or exceeding their sales goals. The stock market is growing. But our beloved country is not ready for the God of justice and peace. I'm pretty sure that the poor didn't make much of an appearance in the new tax bill in D.C. The middle class is there, the rich are there, and the corporations are there. But I don't see any room in our "economic inn" for the poor and the oppressed.

I don't believe we are ready for Christ. For that power, that presence, America is not ready.

My beloved country, we readily comply with our contemporary Augustus, who decrees from a Rome or a Wall Street or a Washington DC, what time of year it is: time to be registered, time to buy, time to sell, time to move, time to be born, time to die. And we comply. Like sheep led to the slaughter.

The world obeyed Rome's decree. Luke tells us that Joseph also went . . . to be registered, and Mary, pregnant with child, went with him. They complied with the decrees of Rome, just as we do. They complied with the culture that calls missiles peacemakers. They complied with a culture that dubs its most deadly weapons as the Mother of All Bombs — we actually christen bombs, the messengers of Thanatos, death, as our mother!

Joseph also went, and Mary with him. Americans also go. To Rome, to be registered, to be taxed, to be exploited, to be deported, or to profit from powers that keep the peace with the sword.

And yet, we know, in our hearts of hearts, that as we go, others weep. As we go, others bleed. As we go. . . .

Tina Forrester of Baltimore — she's one. She's not ready for Christmas. "Eighty-three murders in three months; 172 murders in six months; 336 in 2017, and my husband was No. 334," Tina Forrester said. "I bet you, everybody's Christmas is going to be spectacular, but mine, mine is going to be rifled with despair and the sound of my husband [James Forrester] being murdered over and over and over again. There were four murders the same day as my husband, and then I hear that the city leaders are getting a raise. . . ."[64]

No. 334 James Forrester.

No. 335 Jonathan Tobash.

Savannah Tobash, a soldier in the U.S. Army stationed in Texas, returned to Baltimore on Wednesday. For Christmas you might have thought. Or for mourning, you might have guessed. She is the sister of a young black man, Jonathan "Johnny" Tobash, a Morgan State University student — or he was a student. On Monday night, less than three hours after James Forrester was

---

[64] Lowell Melser and Vanessa Herring, "Police Release Video" on WBAL-TV (22 December 2017) accessed on 4 June 2018 at http://www.wbaltv.com/article/police-release-video-of-persons-of-interest-in-killing-of-musician/1448784

murdered, Jonathan became No. 335. Jonathan was also shot and killed in a robbery.[65]

Are we ready for Christmas? America, my beloved, blood-stained country, are you ready for Christmas?

On Wednesday, in Texas, a six-year old boy, Kameron Prescott, his skin beautiful olive brown, was shot in the stomach when police opened fire on a woman who was suspected of stealing a car. Stealing a car. A car. Four officers opened fire on her as she tried to break into a mobile home. One of those bullets went through the sheet rock thin wall, into that six-year-old boy's stomach.

Dead.

On Thursday . . . just days before Christmas, the story said.

> The sheriff's office kept referring to Kameron as "that young man"[66] — Sheriff, he was a six-year-old *boy*! And now he's dead.

I'm not. Ready.

America, my beloved country, you are not ready. I don't believe America is ready for Christmas. I'd like to cancel it this year. But I can't do that. And somehow, I think it would be wrong to do so. But by the same token, it would be wrong to act as if all is well. As if our biggest dispute is whether we say, "happy holidays" or "merry Christmas". There's blood in our streets and perhaps, if we don't act soon, on our hands.

Perhaps, it would be faithful for us to interrupt the artificial light of this season with the uncreated light of God's promise and presence. To let our joyful anthems be interrupted with mournful lament; to set down our forks full of feasting for a moment; to pray with the hunger of a heart that longs and thirsts for justice; to stop talking small and maybe, for a moment; to open up a big gaping silence at our tables, for people like Kameron's mom, or

---

[65] Kevin Rector, "Morgan State Sophomore Fatally Shot" in *The Baltimore Sun* (21 December 2017) accessed on 4 June 2018 at http://www.baltimoresun.com/news/maryland/crime/bs-md-ci-jonathan-tobash-20171221-story.html.

[66] Ray Sanchez, "Deputies' Stray Bullet Kills Six-Year Old Texas Boy" in *CNN* (23 December 2017) accessed on 4 June 2018 at https://www.cnn.com/2017/12/23/us/texas-deputies-shoot-boy/index.html.

Jonathan's sister, for James' wife . . . for whom it doesn't seem like night will ever end.

All the while, the stock market grows and the tears flow.

Maybe it's time that we interrupted the false peace and false prosperity of the status quo, where we're all alike registered, and interrupt it with the true peace that only Christ can bring. The true peace you find in an animal's stall, in a manger, the true peace that comes *after* labor.

Joseph also went, captive, like the rest of us, to powers over which he had no control. But his going was interrupted by God's coming in Christ. The urgent requirements of labor. That event shifted the world's center. America also goes, registering its compliance with the powers and principalities of this present darkness. But by God's grace, our compliance will be interrupted. Our festivals will be interrupted by the labor pains of those who weep. Our laughter by those who mourn. Our heart's joy, by those who grieve.

By God's grace, our compliance with the sharp labor pains of God's justice, signaling the beginning of the new world, will culminate with the deep joy of a newborn child.

That's the Christmas promise.

Luke is a curiosity as a writer. Luke's narrator will ravish the reader with exquisitely detailed narratives of mercy. It's close up, almost every brush stroke showing the sound of God's mercy. But here, oddly, Luke doesn't record Mary's labor pains — in fact, Luke gives just two verses to the account of Jesus' birth: "The time came for her to deliver the child; she gave birth; wrapped in him bands of cloth; and laid him in a manger because there was no room for them in the inn." That's it. And again, so curious, no labor pains in this story. Why? Could it be because Luke believes that we carry those labor pains in our bodies, this body of believers?

The labor of Christ commands our hearts with the urgency of God's justice in the night half spent; the birth of Christ awakens our hearts with the good news of great joy, for unto you this day, is born a Savior, Emmanuel God with us. The manger is nothing compared to the child, the poverty nothing compared to the love, the suffering nothing compared to the joy. Mary didn't see her poverty. She rejoiced in her firstborn child, her labor complete and her cup overflowing. And yet, everything about God's promise gets gathered up in that manger, a feeding trough for animals. Three times, Luke points to the manger: at Jesus' birth; as sign spoken of by the angel; and the shepherds confirm the revelation by seeing Jesus laying in a manger.

That will be a sign for you that Christmas is near — the labor pains of God's justice.

Where you expected to see a throne, look for a feeding trough. Where you expected to see prosperity, look for poverty. Where you expected to find nothing, see all things, even Christ. Where tears have been your food day and night, making every day into a perpetual night, and every song of joy, a curse of pain, look on high, for our redeemer is near.

Make haste for Christ . . . just as Christ hastens for us. The shepherds heard this message under cover of night, as they labored — but they were surrounded by heavenly light and angel's song. Their night's work interrupted, they went into holy labor, with holy haste to see what the Lord had done in Bethlehem. And, by God's grace, their holy labor produced doxology. The work of mothers who weep, and soldiers who groan, and those who dwell in deep darkness — their work, which is really our work, America's labor pains for justice, will be turned from groans into shouts of joy. So Luke seems to testify.

But first comes the labor, first the contractions of our body with God's justice. First the groan . . . it is a sign for you, for Christ is to be born in us. Maybe we leave one gift unopened on Christmas day. Cry my beloved country, cry for Kameron Prescott, six years-old, child of God, child of the covenant. Cry for his mother, for her child is no more, and she will not be comforted.

Tomorrow is Christmas.

And by God's grace, we won't be ready. . . .

Amen.

December 24, 2017

Chapter Nineteen

Fevers Relieved

The final sermon of this collection moves towards a distinctly Markan theme, namely, that testimony that the rule of God has drawn near. That proclamation disrupts the status quo. What we take as "normal" today is a feverish indifference to the creation, to human dignity, to human suffering. We hear the cries of the children separated from their parents at the border, kept like animals in cages. We hear the grief of mothers who have lost their children to gun violence and poverty. Or, more precisely, perhaps we don't hear our own indifference to those inhuman and ungodly conditions.

The day before this sermon was preached, about one week before Mother's Day, our church hosted between thirty-five and forty women whose children had been killed in Baltimore. Those who gathered were a tiny fraction of those who grieve the loss of well over a thousand people (the overwhelming majority African American) killed in the previous three years in our city. I don't believe I've ever been in a church where more than a few people had been directly impacted by tragedy. And yet, in our church, on that day, being a person who had not lost a child to violence and poverty (which to me are absolutely related) put me in the minority. You could not ignore the magnitude, the gender, or the color of grief in the sanctuary.

Mark's story of Simon and Andrew going home to find their mother in a fever struck me as somehow apt to this text. They didn't expect to find her in a fever; they expected, I suppose, to find her cooking, or as I put it in the sermon, fulfilling her "biblical womanhood" — tongue-in-cheek, of course, but in other ways, I was deadly serious. I feel like God calls us to go deeper into the text or allow the text to go deeper into us. For me, that "deeper" meant attempting to name the fevers not acknowledged, namely, racial and gender constructions which suppress testimony. Tanya Street, one of the mothers, spoke during the service on Saturday. It was not her first time to First & Franklin Church (she also gave the Police Commissioner a purple ribbon in memory of her son), so I knew some of her story already. I visited with her briefly during the luncheon on Saturday. When she spoke to the mothers in the sanctuary, she spoke with courage, conviction, and tenderness; when she spoke with me, afterwards, in the rear chapel, where the luncheon was being held, she also spoke of her inner conflict.

It felt like Mark to me, the way Mark develops the character and inner thoughts of women. It also felt like the way Mark ends, courageous and yet also with a note of ambiguity. We wonder, "What will happen next?"

Sermon

> *As soon as they left the synagogue, they entered the house of Simon and Andrew, with James and John. Now Simon's mother-in-law was in bed with a fever, and they told Jesus about her at once. He came and took her by the hand and lifted her up. Then the fever left her, and she began to serve them.*
>
> — Mark 1:29-39

They knew something was wrong. The house was too quiet. There was no evidence that the woman of the house, Simon's mother-in-law was active, meaning, there were no smells of baking bread, of roasting meat, or stew bubbling away over a fire; there was no, "Come on in boys! Take your shoes off, help yourself to something cool from the fridge" — there were none of the symptoms of the so-called normal life of a biblical woman. You know, the normal life for biblical women serving their biblical version of biblical manhood. But today, something was not normal, seemingly unbiblical, and these disciples, they may not have been the sharpest marbles in the world, but even they detected some departure from normal.

"Mom! Mom! We're home! Mom, what's for dinner? Where are you? Mom? Are you upstairs? She's not answering. I don't where she is. Mom?"

Maybe they had a little ladder leading to an upper room. There weren't many places she could hide. That's the way it was for biblical women. Nowhere to hide! So they climbed the ladder and peered into the dusty place above and saw her shape, maybe they heard her labored breathing.

"Mom, are you okay?" they asked. Groans for answers. Maybe some garbled words. Incoherent. Delusional. Maybe no words at all . . . just the heat radiating off her body, the stifling feeling of no air and no escape.

"It's a fever," they said. "Mom has a fever. She was fine this morning when we left. But now look at her. Feel her, she's hot to the touch! Mom, are you okay? Mom, do you hear me?"

She had a fever. But maybe we know that when our narrator speaks of fevers, it's a symbol. Life can take on a feverish quality. Do you know what that's like? Maybe if you've ever sat up late at night with a loved one, whose is skin is burning up, hot to the touch, whose eyes are glassy and far away, whose body is restless, listless, and fitful, maybe you know the fever of worry, maybe you know how long the night. . . .

If you've ever taken a risk, made yourself vulnerable, you came out to a close friend, or shared your story, your weakness, failures, your pain, and waited for them to say, it's okay, I love you, and accept you, and embrace you, and *you're still waiting, right now, you're still waiting,* maybe you know how long the feverish night.

And you desire wholeness. You seek it. You thirst for it. Pray for it, like the sick who long for health. But what if we don't know we're sick? What if we, like the disciples, take sickness, or not complete wholeness, as certifiably healthy or at least certifiably normal? Isn't that a possibility? That we take sickness as health? Other fevers we may not see as sickness — we may actually applaud them, institutionally and culturally, feeding the fevers. Or maybe the disciples suffered from a fever of gender construction, so commonplace it seemed as if it were engraved in the human condition.

It's not hard to imagine. Fevers of greed seem to be guiding our tax code, rewarding the wealthy and punishing the poor. Fevers of consumerism. Buy more, consume more, drink more. Indulge more. Advertising seems designed to feed the fever of consumerism, not relieve it. Or consider something just as close to home: telling *white lies*, like the fever that would deny white privilege. I'm entitled. I've earned that. I'm not racist even if I benefit from a racist society, a society that is delirious, really, with deadly whiteness. Fevers so familiar they may seem like health. That is, until true health comes to your house. On Saturday, we hosted A Mother's Cry luncheon for the mothers of children killed by gun violence in Baltimore. This sanctuary was filled with black mothers, from mostly black neighborhoods, grieving the deaths of their mostly black children.

Maybe this surprises some of us. But it was kind of hard to miss it on Saturday. As in, at lunch, as we sat around the table, at least one woman could tell you the story of how her son had died, in the street, or how a daughter was shot in the back, murdered for a cell phone. Another woman, perhaps in her forties, used a walker. Turns out she was a victim of a shooting. She was in our church yesterday . . . how accustomed are we to seeing gunshot victims in church? Maybe in a sense, we came home to our church on Saturday and it wasn't normal. Right away something was different. It didn't seem the same. We looked for our mother, and the house seemed unusual, and then we saw her, and she was caught in a fever of unanswerable questions . . . or in the crippling wounds of a drive by shooting ... or in a grief that was still strong, fifteen years on.

Who is sick in this house? Well, grieving mothers seem obvious enough. They're hurting. But if we don't have any empathy, are we really well? It's one thing to be sick. But it's something else again to be indifferent to sickness. I can't imagine sleeping easily while one of our little ones burns with fever ... I would have to be sick, sick, sick to sleep with one of them tossing and turning alone.

Maybe that's something of the point of today's text. Mark's narrative will often place the obviously unwell alongside the systemically unwell. And, in Mark's gospel, it often turns out that those who knew they were ill were ready to accept Jesus' healing; but those who are partially well but profoundly sick are the most resistant to healing.

And, therefore, healing for them comes more slowly, if at all. Maybe that's the disciples, the partially, not completely unwell. The disciples didn't know what was happening; their world was in danger, or at least what they took to be their world was in danger, of changing. And maybe they felt a fever of anxiety.

They went to Jesus, desperate to have Jesus return the world to its original, normal operating condition. "Hurry," they said, "Mom's not doing so good." Jesus didn't rebuke them for being blind to their own fevers. He could have done, but he didn't. Instead, Jesus went to her, and he touched her, and she was healed. She got up and began to *serve* them — that seems like everything got back to normal, biblical womanhood restored, doesn't it? Like she freshened up, whipped up a nice Sunday dinner. And the boys got to be boys again, just like before, just like normal. You could conclude that Simon's mother-in-law is a flat character, no name, disappears into the background. We never see her again. She might as well still be in the house, cooking stew. You could say that. Many have. Yet, if we look closely and at the way Mark portrays women characters in the larger story, we might see something more interesting.

According to Susan Miller, a feminist scholar, in the broad sweep of Mark's story, our narrator will praise women as "models" of faithful action, especially in their willingness to cross social boundaries. But Jesus will also praise what women say — not just what they do. She also notes something distinctive to Mark: unlike other characters in Mark's gospel, we will hear the internal, unfiltered thoughts of women, their ambivalence as well as their trust in God — Jesus doesn't hear those thoughts; the characters in the story don't hear those thoughts; but we, audience of Mark, do hear those thoughts. And because we hear their inner testimony, we connect with their transparency, their complexity, their authenticity.[67] Remember the women on the way to the tomb? "Who will remove the stone for us?" That was for us. That's our question, too. We recognize that. And Mark ends with an ambivalent note about women as well: they fled from the tomb and said nothing to anyone because they were afraid. Kind of like real life, don't you think?

That's the larger narrative arc. Today's text inaugurates that journey towards wholeness. Our narrator says that she served them using the Greek word Mark uses when he depicts the angels ministering to Christ while he was in the wilderness.

Angels. Mark compares her to an angel. You know what an angel is, right? Maybe we think of the angels in Christmas plays, cute children. Nothing against cute children in angel costumes. But in Scripture, an angel is a messenger, a preacher, or one who bears witness. An angel speaks as a pillar of fire. Pillar of fire. She soars, she creates her own weather system, she breathes in and roars out. You meet an angel, and you're first thought isn't going to be, "What's for dinner?" Or, "Isn't she cute!" It's going to be a sense of awe, that you're in the presence of some power, some messenger, some truth teller . . . she's preparing to speak.

Her sermon was brilliant, by the way. She was articulate. She was profound. I was *so* moved by what she said. "Wow," I thought, "she can preach!" I was in my second of year of seminary, had more hair than sense, and I wanted to meet her, this powerful, intelligent, incisive woman. And so, after church, I waited in line until it was my turn to greet the preacher. And then I saw her, and I was shocked:

"But you're so short!" I said.

I'm embarrassed now, but I guess I expected her to be at least eighteen-feet tall, the way she preached. In reality, she was maybe on the high side of four feet. It turns out she had been standing on a booster in a pulpit that had been designed for someone more like me.

And I realized, belatedly, that I wasn't supposed to say that sort of thing to such a distinguished personage, which she was. So I said, "I'm sorry, I didn't

---

[67] Susan Miller, "Women Characters in Mark's Gospel" in Christopher W. Skinner and Matthew Ryan Hauge, eds., *Character Studies and the Gospel of Mark* (New York: Bloomsbury T&T Clark, 2014), 174-193.

mean that, but you're such a powerful preacher! I never imagined you would be *so* short" — I was just digging my hole deeper and deeper by the second.

Truly, I don't know if she was offended or complimented, or amused, or puzzled by my reaction, but maybe, in my own defense, I was coming out of a fever where only men preach, tall men, with big voices, and egos to go with them. But now, I wonder if I was listening to a granddaughter of Simon's mother-in-law, and she was releasing me from a fever that I did not know that I had — and she had done so not by being my nurse, but by being a messenger of good news that day. She was a pillar of fire, about 4'10" tall. And my heart began to turn, *and I didn't know it needed to turn*, but it did.

Sometimes fevers make you see things, say things, believe things that just aren't true. And sometimes, truth surprises us . . . or turns us in a more compassionate way, towards healing, reconciliation, and the good news of God's rule.

What might it take for us to turn to the good news of God in Jesus Christ? To be surprised by the surprising *stature* of good news? Perhaps it means acknowledging that if black mothers are grieving the loss of their babies, and that doesn't bother us, then we're sick people, feverishly sick.

But I've got to say, I do feel as if God's Spirit is surprising us these days. Maybe like the disciples, the fever is beginning to lift — not all at once, but in fits and starts — because when those mothers gather in one house, that is a strong house, a Spirit-filled house, and it's likely to create its own weather system, a movement in which a solitary groan can turn, by God's grace, into a whirlwind of saving health in our city.

Tanya Street spoke about her son, Sherman Caruthers, killed outside their home in February 2017. Maybe, in any other house, she would grieve silently. Maybe, in any other house, she would drink her cup of tears alone. Maybe, in any other house . . . but in this house, she stood up, heart aching with true speech, and she testified. She testified that she had her arguments with God. Why? Why my son? Why me? And she testified that God spoke to her in the still small quiet voice of the Spirit. That her loss was not in vain. That God was at work. She testified to her sisters that they were not alone.

"Tanya," I said, "you gave us a good word today."

And she said, "You know, it wasn't scary at all . . . I just spoke, and the words came." But then her last words, almost like words spoken to herself, words that I overheard: "Now I think I'm going to go home and cry. . . ."

You wonder, as she flees the tomb under a fever of grief, will she speak again, will ever tears be stilled . . . she might speak, they might be stilled. By God's grace and to God's glory, she may . . . we may. . . .

Amen.

May 6, 2018

www.ingramcontent.com/pod-product-compliance
Lightning Source LLC
Chambersburg PA
CBHW052145110526
44591CB00012B/1866